Songs From The River

Reflections From The Spaces Between My Thoughts

Theodore Slipchinsky

ISBN:
ISBN-13: 9780692522080

DEDICATION

To Kathy Gessay, my dearest and oldest soul friend, who incarnates at those moments when the greatest strength is needed.

To the Vibration of Light which is all that is.

CONTENTS

ACKNOWLEDGMENTS

To the many friends who have graciously asked me to assemble my writings into book form; I thank you for your love and support. I also acknowledge those who have offered me encouragement and feedback over the years, by commenting on my Facebook posts, particularly the members of the various Anita Moorjani Discussion groups. Your words were a balm to my creative process and provided me with the encouragement I needed to express my soul in the world.

INTRODUCTION

One day, over twenty years ago, I sent out a cry to the Universe. I asked to feel more alive, to remove the band of suppression which for so long had clouded my consciousness. The answer to my call was so intense, it felt as if I might be losing my mind. The Stillness, which inhabits the spaces between my thoughts, came alive as a dynamic vibrating energy.

At first it seemed as if some alien force was invading my being. In time I began to see that this energy was offering me the gift of my own essence. It was presenting me with the opportunity to grow beyond the shrunken facsimile of self, which I had been conditioned to think was who I was, into a far grander awareness.

My cry had been answered. Never in my wildest dreams did I think that this answer would set in motion a process which would continue to this very day. The vibrating foundational energy which I first felt over twenty years ago, has never shut off. Through trial and error - through fear, stubbornness and surrender – I continue to learn to integrate this force into my consciousness and my physical body.

It has not been easy. In addition to expanding joy and purpose, I have managed to create my fair share of pain and dis-ease (not from the energy itself, but from my fear of letting it flow).

The reflections, stories, teachings and songs in this book come from the place inhabited by this accelerated energy; "the river" which flows through the spaces between my thoughts. Most took the form of Facebook posts put up over a three year period. They are not intended as absolute truth, but as one man's experience. As the Divine energy eroded the walls that I had built around my heart, words began to flow like the river from which they came; words mingled with tears at the memory of the One Heart. I offer these words to you now. It is my hope that they give you strength in these incredible days that are upon us.

I. REFLECTIONS

#1 The River

There is a river that runs through my being, a mighty current that courses through the spaces between my thoughts. It has always been and always will be, a living spark of All That Is . Upon its surface dance my human emotions, at times flowing in ceaseless harmony, at times congealing into dams of muck and stone, or whirlpools that turn madly in upon themselves.

But the river is not deterred. It casts aside all barriers, all perceptions of security. Resting in Divine perfection, even as it moves, it smashes the dams and tears apart the eddies.

I bow to the great river of life which flows through all. With gratitude I surrender to its flow, knowing that we are One.

#2 Our New Clothes

My friends, a new energy is upon us. Some of you may feel it. It is like a wonderful new set of clothes. As soon as you put these clothes on you are overcome with the urge to dance! You look in the mirror and find that you are ten years younger. As you get used to these garments, you discover your aches, pains and sadness falling away. Make no mistake, these are magical clothes that engender broad smiles, tender insights, and bursts of outrageous laughter.

Little did we know how terribly dull and restrictive our old outfits were. This is because, no matter how well they were made, they lacked magic. Our new clothes are infused with the alchemy of Spirit, for this is where they were forged. They are free of course. We have earned the right to wear them through our desire, our perseverance, and our tears.

I have seen old men and women, twirling elegantly around the ballroom floor, their broad smiles full of delight. "This is our birthright," they whisper. "Come join the dance. You already have everything you need. All that must be done now is to live fearlessly. And this you shall surely do, my friend, this you shall surely do."

#3 Sleep Well, My Friend

Sleep well tonight my friend, wrapped in the sweet blanket of self-acceptance. Those who were with you when you were born, a star burst forth from the Great Divine, are with you now and hold you in the highest honor. Their love will never fail. Even as they shed a tear for the challenges that you face, they know well your courage and see you flowing into the joy and the peace which you deserve.

Wrap yourself in their love. Let the angels sing their praises of you; of the soul who came to earth and did her very best to remember who she was, when so many others were content to forget. And with her remembrance, she lit up the world. Yes, please sleep well and understand that all challenges pass, all dreams of the soul are realized; and you are held and cherished by the universe. Om Shanti Om. Peace to all beings.

#4 Don't Despair

Please don't despair. Your blessed guidance is closer now than it ever has been. You can reach out and touch it if you let yourself.

The hard times and the confusion only mean that the old, worn strategies are falling away. They reach their crescendo and they pass. When the baby bird is pushed from the nest, in one moment it seems to her that all is lost, then with the first faltering flutter of her wing, she knows that she can soar. And so can we. Here. In this place of wood and stone.

You have so much to teach, so much to share - not above any other - but with the deepest humility, for who can touch another's heart better than one who has been lost in the darkness and the pain? Please do not withhold from yourself the kindness that you so freely give to strangers.

There is no limit to your love. That which you call God, which is far greater than your conception could ever be, loves and honors you in all its Infinite power. For you come from the Holy of Holies. This is who you are.

So please, through all your trials, rejoice. For your pain will most surely end, and dissolve into endless bliss.

#5 The Holy Of Holies

I have gone through many emotions, watching and listening to the nightmare events that endlessly unfold in this world. I have been cold and unyielding. I have been numb. I have been rational. I have been scared. I have been hateful. I have been every place, it seems, except the one place where I feel most real; my own heart.

"Only a fool would claim to take refuge in his heart during times like these," whispers the ego. "Do you choose to invite catastrophe upon your head? The world is in turmoil. It is everyone for himself. How is your heart going to save you?" I answer with tears. With tears I enter The Holy of Holies, the abode of the Divine within me.

And in its arms I shall rest forever.

#6 A Message From The Earth

The yard in front of the cabin is filled with the clarity of a crisp December evening. The air is alive with a wondrous sense of expectancy. The earth awaits the first snowfall of the season like a lover holding space for her beloved.

I allow my body to be caressed by the deep order of the earth. My thoughts turn to the love that underlies all things. Mother Earth whispers that every rock, every snowflake, every human entanglement is an expression of love, the very breath of God.

"How did I manage to forget again?" I wonder. "How did my eyes become clouded and my heart obscured?"

"Never mind," The Mother replies. "Stand upon me, breathe, and I shall always remind you."

I laugh at the simplicity of it all.

Once again I fall asleep in Her arms.

#7. God Can Indeed Cure Anything

God can indeed cure anything. As long as you understand that it is the sacred energy of your being, and all it wants to do is flow.

#8 The Mountain Top

I too have been to the mountain top. There I looked out over the great vastness of the world and yearned to express; to write, to sing, to share all that I feel when I rest in the lap of love, held by the Source of all.

I bow to that Source. Without servitude, I bow. I know that all it desires is for me to soar, and to return to it with the knowledge of my flight. It smiles at my bows and the stars brighten with joy. It sees beyond my self-loathing, my insanity, my endless fears into that which I am; a spark it gave birth to and has always cherished. How many troubles would be spared if only we remembered the love you have for every one of us, and that indeed, we are this very love? How could we lift our hand to strike another when we saw you standing there before us? For you are the essence of love, you seed the universe with love, you create all life with love.

Once again I bow. You whisper within my heart, "My son. You are as limitless as I."

#9 **Dear Brother**

Dear Brother:

I will meet you by the fire in the deep forest clearing where judgment dies, in the place the women have been nurturing since time began. You may leave your sword behind; you will not need it here.

This is the place your soul longs for and your mind fears above all others. What I have I offer freely, for here there is only abundance. All are cherished by the Mother.

The beasts you once slaughtered will approach you without fear. They will let you caress them and be on their way.

In this place you can rest and restore yourself. Here you will find the true energy of life; not in your books or your temples, but in the spaces between your thoughts.

Look about you. Look at what your mind and emotions, divorced from Source, have wrought; the self-righteousness, the fear, the hatred of those who are different. You have even managed to convince yourself that your brutal ways are somehow blessed by God!

The Mother awaits you patiently and offers you the balance you have sought. She no longer hides in caves and shadows but has come to claim what is rightfully hers.

Come down to the campfire, my brother. We will weep together for what has been, and rejoice for what is being born.

#10 Embrace The Future

Embrace the future, my friend, you have nothing to fear in the expansion of your soul. Indeed, it is what you came here for.

If someone seeks to keep you small, bless them, and take refuge in the knowledge that by allowing your soul to bloom, you always serve the highest good of all. For those who cling to seeing you through their own limited vision, know that by lovingly shattering that vision, you help them to expand into the beauty of their own being.

Fear nothing, for you are the creator of worlds.

You are a spark of All That Is on a journey of remembering. Every experience you have serves Creation, and there is never a moment when you are not held in measureless love.

#11 I Bow To The Terror

I bow to the terror within me, for it is part of All That Is. From the darkened shadows I call it forth. With open arms I stand before it and with sacred breath I draw it unto me.

The terror softens, for at long last it is seen for what it is; the child who in my ignorance and fear, was long ago banished from the kingdom of my consciousness.

I bow to the terror within me and welcome it home. It accepts my bow, and graciously offers me the gift of wholeness.

#12 I Hear You

I have made the wrong choices thousands and thousands of times. I have stood at the gates of Heaven and recoiled at the headwinds of fear. I have raced blindly into the gaping caverns of my mind's deceptions, like an insect careening into a spider's deathly embrace. There I awoke, time and time again, bleeding and yearning for the balm of your presence.

In one breath I called and I cursed you; but I could never hear you when you answered me. Where were you God/Goddess of my dreams; vibrating out on the furthest reaches of the universe? You dwelled in the one place where my fear would not grant me entrance; my own beating heart. I hear you now, Beloved, in the silence, in the falling leaves, in the still spaces between my thoughts.

I hear you.

#13 Forgiveness

Forgiveness is not about bestowing a gift upon another.

It is about freeing ourselves from those thoughts and emotions which obscure our true magnificence.

In this sense, it is the most profound gift that we can ever give ourselves.

#14 The River Of Life

Well I am back in my canoe again, floating down the river of Creation. The river has been very profound of late, as I allow it to overtake me. It vibrates and pulsates with the unfolding of my soul's design. At age sixty-five, I am younger now, and far more excited than I was when I was eighteen.

When I was eighteen I was burdened by the torments and whispers of my ego-based mind. Nobody ever taught me that I was magnificent; that I was a flowing droplet in the great river of life.

They taught me algebra. They taught me that God was up there, unapproachable, craving to be worshiped. They taught me that I wasn't good looking or athletic enough to be loved. But no, they never taught me that I was magnificent. Now I know, because I am a part of the river and the river is magnificence in its purest form. I and the river are One. I wish to shout this from the highest mountain ledges. I wish to watch the trees sway in acknowledgment and hear the birds sing in delight at my exclamation.

There are still "lessons" to be learned. The mind holds sway at times with its trembling demands for acceptance and survival. I know that I need but lovingly bless these thoughts and return them to the great river of peace. I know, I know, but I don't really know; at least not at all levels of my being. And that is perfectly fine.

The river knows. It has nothing to prove. It seeks only to expand and to serve. Form and consequence have no meaning to it. Past, present and future are expressed in every sacred moment of its flow. The river allows but never molds. It seeks only to celebrate, and this, my friends, is the true meaning of worship.

#15 **The World That I Am Of**

Lately I am truly glad that I am in this world but not of it. I have journeyed to the world that I am of. It is a world where compassion rules over a realm of indescribable Grace.

This is where I come from. This is where you come from. This is where we always are. This is where we shall return soon enough. We can draw strength from this magnificent realm which gave birth to our souls. Nurtured by the boundless energy of All That Is, we can serve in this human dream of blood and bone, with hearts full of joy and gratitude, even as we walk among its sorrows.

#16 **The Face Of God**

As a child I thought if I could touch the sky, I would touch the face of God. As a man I learned that all I had to do was touch my own heart.

#17 **The World Is Waiting For You**

The time has come to do what your soul yearns to do. If you continue to delay, to make excuses for not singing that song, painting that painting, planting that garden, volunteering with those dying patients - for not sharing what you wish to share from the very deepest part of your being - then you will end up making yourself miserable without ever knowing why. These ruts can grow very deep. No amount of will power may be able to get you out of them, and they can get filled in with all kinds of symptoms.

The mind always has a great excuse: "they'll think I'm nuts," "I have no talent," "who would want to hear what I have to say," "I can't afford it," and the eternal, "everything's got to be perfect before I try."

Then of course, you can rant and rave about all those people who are trying to dominate you (not that such people don't exist, they have always existed); but this becomes the all encompassing hole into which you bury your creative energies. It is a highly effective technique of the fear-based ego to keep you from facing your fears and sharing your soul in the world.

I was once told by some wise channeled friends that I am constantly thinking that the world has to get its act together before it is safe for me to express my soul in it; when actually it is the world which is waiting for me.

The world is waiting for you. It needs millions of awakening beings, each doing what excites and ignites them. So sing your song, dance your dance, paint your masterpiece, make your garden, become the healer you were afraid to become.

The world is waiting for you. And in the process you may find that your sadness is lifted and your body made whole.

#18 Resurrection!

To be resurrected is to align with the current of your own being; to that which flows through you, beneath your thoughts, emotions and beliefs. This is what you are. This is the God you pray to. This is the One you were always taught lies outside of you. This is the Force which bestows all blessings - not by beseeching it from without - but by daring to claim it as that which you truly are.

You are the river of life! You are the stars and the Heavens. You are The One that always has been and always will be. You are the Perfection. Every pain that you endure bears this message. Every obstacle you face brings you to this understanding.

#19 **The Wave**

My God is not some being in a far off Heaven, but a wave that washes upon me with each intake of breath, and returns to shore with each exhale. He requires no worship. Indeed, he worships me by filling me with his holy essence.

His only sacrament is the deep acceptance of Self.

#20 **Everything Is Created By Self**

Everything is ordained and created by self. Everything, no matter how horrific it may seem was called forth because you called it forth, and everything serves the longing of your soul to grow.

When you realize this, all you can do is fall down in gratitude; gratitude that you are so loved by Creation, that God/Goddess would never prevent you from travelling the path which you yourself have chosen.

My Prayer

I bow to Creation, to the One of which I AM.
I ask the Helpers to help me to understand why I create the paths which I create.
I proclaim that every moment, every breath, is Creation's moment, Creation's breath, and that my joy comes in realizing that I AM a part of All That Is.

There is nothing that could ever make me less than Creation.

When in frailty and in fear, I forget,
May I be helped to remember.

When in pride I look away
Let me be taught gracefully.

Let me know you
Let me touch you
Let me live you
Let me be you

Amen

#21 **The Circle**

Come with me now, let us form a circle. Let us hold hands and remember what we are.

Whoever is inspired to enters the center of the ring. We on the outside let our love flow into you, focusing on the perfect Divinity of your soul. We acknowledge that we are of the Light, and that there is no separation. Then one at a time, more and more of us move into the center. We dance together gracefully as one organism.

Suddenly a miraculous event! Our bodies disappear and all that is left is a ring of shimmering light, more magnificent than any of us have ever witnessed. It is made of many smaller lights that weave in and through one another in a dance of cosmic joy. We are lost in the ecstasy of essence.

And the angels bow their heads in gratitude.

#22 The Path To Peace

The great irony of the ego is that it always expresses our sense of unworthiness. Lurking beneath the mask of bravado is the kid nobody wanted on their baseball team, the boy who was bullied at summer camp, the young man the girls thought was weird; the one who retreated into a world far removed from the every day slights he perceived around him.

The boy grows up, but the child still longs to be heard. He cannot rejoice at the success of others because he is blinded by the illusion of his own incompleteness. He wants to be recognized because he believes that only by standing out from the crowd will he finally be seen. He must raise his voice above the others or he will disappear.

One day he hears the still small voice of his own soul calling. It is the memory of his true magnificence, that part of him which does not need to be special, but wishes only to share. It makes itself known in his moments of gravest discomfort. Its whispers remain when all the accolades, possessions, and substances can no longer overwhelm his sorrow.

Slowly, inexorably - through intention and trial - the man learns to listen, respect, and live from the seed of his own being. He no longer needs to smash anyone down, to bedazzle and confuse with his mind, to dominate or to destroy. He learns to rest in the great, majestic river of his own Divinity. He is at peace.

#23 Heart

I can make things as complicated as I like, but one fact remains. The most real place I know is in my own heart. When my heart opens and I feel compassion; I feel the most real, the most like who I truly am.

All the machinations of my mind are pale imitations.

And only fear can lead me to forget.

#24 **Prayer**

I do not pray in church or temple to a God beyond. I ask the breath of life to flow freely from my crown to my feet into the sweet earth.

In this movement the Divine reveals itself to me as that which I am.

#25 **The Lord's Prayer Interpreted**

Our father, which art in heaven,
Hallowed be thy name

Mother/Father, Source of All
That which inhabits the Unseen
And dwells within
Each human heart

You are Holy beyond measure
As are we, for we are of your essence

The Masters whisper your Glory
With the deepest humility,
The profoundest joy
And the greatest gratitude.

Thy kingdom come.
Thy will be done in earth,
As it is in heaven.

Your kingdom has never left us,
In truth it comes again

As we let go of fear
And are filled with your sacred essence.

In this way is the prophecy realized
"As above so below"
And Heaven on Earth is made manifest.

Give us this day our daily bread.
And forgive us our trespasses,
As we forgive them that trespass against us.

All that we need to sustain ourselves is drawn to us
When we fill ourselves with the Divine Energy
Which we are a part of

The self-love born of aligning with All That Is
Bestows forgiveness upon us
In our joy we understand the true meaning of forgiveness.
That there never was anything to forgive
Because in joy there is no need to forgive

And lead us not into temptation,
But deliver us from evil.

As we become consciously filled with our own Divinity
The "temptations" of the grosser energies
Dissolve into bliss

We observe and accept that which the world calls "evil"
And allow it to pass through us
For we have touched a deeper truth
We have touched our essence

For thine is the kingdom,
The power, and the glory,
For ever and ever.
Amen.

All power, all glory, all kingship

Lies in the Divine life force
Our eternal reality
Which no power on earth can destroy
Amen

#26 A Man Who Once Called Himself Ted

A man who once called himself "Ted" sits in the space of non-thought. It dawns on him that this is a space between worlds; a void between the strutting, delusional certainty of the ego, and the unimaginable joy of the soul. The man never did well with the former and always turned back in fear from the latter.

The dog stares at him with radiant eyes. She senses something, but knows that this is a road only humans must walk.
Is this what it means to quit fighting, when mind and body say "enough," when something ancient whispers, "take me dear river of life, whatever you are, wherever you wish to go. I can fight you no longer, nor can I ever hope to understand you."

 I no longer fear the death of this man. I offer him freely unto you.

#27 A Visit From An Angel

One day I awoke to find that I had built a cage around myself. I ran from one wall to the next and banged on the bars but they would not budge. So I went to the center of the cage and sat down in the dirt and cried.

Suddenly an angel appeared. She looked at me with eyes that held all of the love in the universe. Then she knelt down next to me.

"Why do you weep," she asked?

I looked away and stammered, "Can't you see, I am trapped in this cage. Everywhere I go there are bars."

The angel smiled and a million stars grew brighter. She waved her arm and a majestic river came down from the heavens, through the bars on the top of the cage, and flowed into my heart. I closed my eyes and felt a joy beyond measure.

"This is what you are, my friend," the angel said.

"This river of light will carry you beyond all of the cages that you can ever construct with your mind. Whenever the illusion tells you there is no way out, you have but to breathe deeply, accept what you feel, and allow the river to encompass you. Know that I will always be there, waiting to embrace you."

With these words, the angel rose, spread her wings, and drew me unto her. I felt a love a million times stronger than the love of a mother for her child. I surrendered to this love and vowed never to imprison myself again.

#28 **The Dance Of Life**

There is a certain softness that comes over you when you make peace with the darkness you believe exists within yourself. Like the prodigal son, the banished parts of your being are welcomed home, to warm themselves beside the sacred fire of your core. The fire rejoices and burns brightly, as it beckons its beloved children back unto itself. For indeed it has been said, "let the darkness suggest the light." The darkness comes, seeking only to be transformed; but first it must be fully seen, illuminated by the sacred fire.

Only then can the dance of life begin.

#29 If Fear Shows Up

If fear shows up at the doorstep of your consciousness, bow deeply to it and thank it for showing you the path to your liberation. If it tells you that by fully feeling it you will die, then by all means breathe into it, die, and be reborn.

#30 Whispers

Whenever the mind starts to weave its subtle overlays of expectation and fear - so that the sacred current of life seems unapproachable– it is often only the body's unhappy response to these seductive whispers which gets our attention.

I listen to my blessed body and surrender to the blissful uncertainty of All That Is. Back in my canoe, on the river of life once again, I marvel at how the distance between sorrow and joy is but the blinking of an eye; the subtle shifting of a thought.

#31 Should I Fear Death?

Should I fear falling into the all compassionate embrace of the Light of Creation? Should I fear the love which is beyond all measure, which ignites every particle of my soul? Should I fear effortless flight, the rebirth of wings, the dawning of joy, the return of laughter, the rekindling of passion and the release of pain? Should I fear the grand homecoming, the joyful reunion with those long thought forever gone?

No, I will embrace this gift, this dream called life; but when death comes I pray that I may embrace it too, and greet this dear friend with joyous anticipation.

#32 The Heart

Your heart will connect with people that your mind refuses to let in. It doesn't mean you have to accept anybody's belief system. The heart accepts that everyone's belief system is perfect, for them.

After that little truth is established, all the heart wants to do is dance.

#33 Again The River

I am feeling the river once again, its deep currents flowing through the spaces between my thoughts. For a while I had cast a shroud over it, as I terrorized myself with my own mind. Release from the prison I forged came when I summoned the courage to do what was simplest yet most profound; to allow myself to experience the fear - not to deny, run, magnify or nurture it - but to simply feel it. The result was another miracle.

Feeling the fear, breathing into it, is the price of admission to the great river of life. Once we do this, we discover how simple it was all along. The Observer Self, the one who feels the fear, flows naturally into the sacred waters. There is space now, space between being and illusion. The remnants of the mind's terrors inexorably lose their charge. We are free.

Over and over again, I teach myself that there is no other path, but the path of surrender to All That Is.

#34 Guru Luna

My dog Luna is my Guru. She has the art of being down to perfection. She has maintained a vow of silence her entire life. She never gives advice, but radiates unconditional love. She always tries to teach by example. From her I am slowly learning how to be in the now, how to live exuberantly, how to express my true feelings, how to be joyful, how to deal with loss, how to love, and a host of other virtues. I know I am a slow learner, but Guru Luna has infinite patience. All her teachings are offered freely, and she is known to bestow frequent kisses upon her disciples.

#35 Alive

It is not from the swirling whirlpool of thought and emotion that I draw the deepest truth of my being, but from that force which lies, perpetually unperturbed, beneath the chaos. One day you realize that you are not the debris that churns madly about on the surface of the river, but the river itself. You do not rail against the debris; but you rest in the sublime truth of your own essence.

You no longer seek to love because you have become love. You no longer have expectations, yet you are filled with a sense of joyful expectancy. You delight as you observe your deepest yearnings fulfilled without the least bit of striving.

You are alive within the glorious majesty of being.

#36 To The Child Who Burns

I cannot save you. I cannot wrap my arms around you and make the flames stop burning your skin. I cannot tell your leaders or those who oppose them to find a better way, for they will not listen. I cannot tell my own leaders anything. They don't know me. I am nothing to them. They will not listen either. But you, you are everything to me. You are the son I never had, the younger brother I never got to see grow up. You are the child of an ancient culture. What have we done, all of us, to set you afire? What have we done?

All I can do is bow my head before you, for I know that you are my teacher. Your flames burn into the hearts of millions, forcing us to come to grips with the madness of our ways. My own heart cries, "how many burning children will it take before we turn to the Love which is our essence, and the essence of the Gods we worship and their prophets? How many?" I do not want to stay here. I do not want to watch you burn.

But I have work yet still to do. You are everything to me. So I will stay and do my work.

#37 **Everlasting Life**

Let others debate the nature of the Unseen. I stand within the pillar of Light that gives me life. I allow that light to seep deeply into all the cells of my body and down into the sweet earth.

Everlasting life does not come from the machinations of the mind but from the energy of All That Is flowing freely.

It is not by reaching out to God, but by bringing God down through me, that my dreams are realized. The body longs to feel the dance of life in every cell. I ride the wave of sacred breath into joy.

#38 **A Simple Prayer For Every Day**

Please help me to choose love over fear, truth over illusion, and to consciously feel and express my own true nature.

Amen.

#39 **It Gets Better**

It gets better my friends. It truly does. The thoughts and emotions which torment you today become distant echoes, and one day they dissolve into that great shimmering ocean of Divinity which is what you are. They lose all potency, all charge, all the power that they never really had.

No, this is not death; you remain in this vessel of blood and bone, buoyed by the sacred current of your being. Isn't this what you deserve, to experience the holy rhythm of your own life force? The purpose you so earnestly yearn for unfurls before you with the simplicity of breath. No hidden gymnastics, no secret formulas, no blind obedience to any teacher or creed; just your own magnificence inexorably unfolding before you.

You want to fall to your knees in gratitude; but the current lifts you up and tells you that the greatest gratitude is in rejoicing. Indeed, your rejoicing is felt to the furthest corners of the universe; into the realms of angels, in spaces which you never dreamed existed.

The Light rejoices with you.

For you are One.

#40 **For Those Who Suffer**

You who sit at the edge of the river of despair, who drink each day from it's darkened waters; you are my teachers. I have known a small measure of the pain that you endure, and railed against the Gods like a deranged fool. There you sit with beauty, grace and dignity, thanking others for their kindness, freely offering your blessings, sharing your gratitude for the gifts you still count every day.

Be ever so gentle with your own true self. If my words were eagles they would seize your pain in their mighty talons and lift it away to a distant land. But all I can give you are my blessings; the love of one who knows that we are brothers and sisters born of the same Oneness.

It is all I have to give.

#41 Mind And Soul

Your mind looks out upon the world and sees a desperate array of problems that you cannot begin to solve. Your soul sees endless beauty. Your mind, and its handmaiden, fear, pile one burden on top of the other, until your life force is almost depleted. Your soul, and its handmaiden, heart, fill you with an endless bounty of joy and compassion as deep as the universe. Which do you choose to believe?

Why not drink from the well of Infinite Life which is your birthright? This does not mean denying the world. It means being truly alive in the world. This does not mean running from suffering. It means being fully engaged in the alleviation of suffering.

The mind is but an imperfect tool.

It was never meant to be your Master.

#42 A Truly Momentous Event

Something truly momentous happened to me today, although the entire event took all of three seconds. I was putting a label on a CD (the one with the photo of me talking to a large wooden statue of St. Francis). As I was affixing the label, I looked down at my face, and from some hidden place came the words, "what a nice man!"

This might sound strange, even trivial, but for me hearing these words was a revelation; an opening to a deep, heretofore unrecognized wellspring. To be able to look at my face and genuinely say (and more importantly to feel) these words seemed life changing. It has taken me 65 years to be able to say this about myself; and even as I write this, part of me wants to cry.

I also feel some embarrassment, and I am aware of how deeply conditioned we are not to love ourselves. Part of me shrinks from this simple act of self-acceptance. But on a deeper level there is a great sense of relief; that I can finally look at myself and feel the goodness in what I see, instead of recoiling.

It is my sincere wish that we all may see beyond the fearful masks we wear into the inherent beauty of our souls.

#43 Some Thoughts About Fear

It is not in the lofty, soaring spaces of our consciousness where we break the chains that bind us. It is in the darkened reaches of the basement, under the rotten floor boards; in the long forgotten crevices, where the snakes and spiders rule. These forbidding places will suggest the light, if we but allow them to; but first they must be acknowledged and welcomed to the table. When we learn to embrace our deepest, darkest fears with the simple grace of being, they lose all power over us.

For indeed, we are the gods who created them.

#44 The God Of Love

What can I do but surrender to the God of Love?

A young man wears a dress and dances on the side of the street. He has done you no harm, yet you tell me that you want to throw him in the river to drown. I look into your eyes and I see the little girl who was taught that only a select few were worthy of her love. To love those deemed unworthy was dangerous and would make her weak. I see this little girl shrinking, taking on her parents' hate like a poisonous suit of armor.

It was not her fault. She was too young to know the difference and she needed her parents' love to survive; so she absorbed the hate that came with it. She decided long ago whom it was safe to love, and who threatened her so badly that she needed to hate them.

You, sir, tell me the people on food stamps are destroying the country. I can feel the hatred in your voice. I look into your eyes and see your sorrow. It is a bottomless sorrow which has entangled your heart like a grotesque weed. I want to tell you that this is an invasive weed, not native to your being. But I know you are not ready to hear me. I see your long forgotten dreams; surrendered to the belief that life is struggle. Dear friend, your rage has nothing to do with the unfortunate people on food stamps, but with the joy that you abandoned long ago.

I do not hate you. Oh my mind could come up with a thousand reasons to do so. Self righteousness is the most seductive of drugs. It would be easy for me to join the chorus. But I will not become part of this mob. I will surrender to the God of Love, which is what we are, and which is all that is real.

Together with those who join me, we are changing the world.

#45 **The Dragon**

I lay down my sword before the fire breathing dragon of fear. Bowing low I kiss its ancient brow.

"Thank you," I murmur, as I caress its gnarled and knotted horn.

"You have shown me the road to liberation. You have humbled me with purifying flames. Here, in the dust, shorn of armor and weapons, I can finally see you; my brother, child of Light, cloaked in holiness."

Only when I truly look into your eyes can I embrace the jewel of my own essence.

#46 **The Flowering**

How can I describe the unfolding of the design of my soul? For years I have heard the concept, but it was only a concept; far off and unknowable. Now, by some unfathomable Grace, I can feel my soul flowering before me. I can sense it, taste it, breathe into it; the birth of the most eternal part of my being, here in this world of blood and bone. No I cannot fill in the details. I don't need to. Only the mind craves details. The heart comes alive and dances, knowing that dreams long abandoned are being reawakened, relationships long forgotten are being reborn, and creative expressions long forsaken are being rekindled. All that the soul yearns for, to express and to serve in this world, is becoming real.

And the beauty of it is, there is nothing to do - nothing at all, except what is right in front of my nose - simply be true to the ever expanding force that flows through me, and allow all that my soul desires to be drawn unto it.

The old man dances at night in the barren field; his arms upraised, his head lifted in eternal bliss. He no longer cares what the naysayers think, nor what words are uttered by those whose minds are clogged with the refuse of their thoughts. The Great Mother holds him tightly in her arms. Together they twirl in an ecstatic embrace - until the whole world disappears - and all that is left is the sound of their laughter, echoing in the emptiness.

#47 **Love**

If I could give the world but one message, if I could plant one seed in every beating heart; it would be this: do not judge. Become one with the magnificent vibrancy of All That Is, and watch your

28

judgments fade like mist. Then rejoice at your newfound freedom, for in place of judgment is born a sense of Oneness with all life. The urge to judge dissolves because you are no longer afraid. You have created a garden within your own consciousness that allows your heart to bloom, and your heart seeks only union with everyone and everything.

How many times, in how many eras, and in how many lands do our poets and our prophets need to remind us of the centrality of love? The answer echoes off the mountain tops; until we learn.

And we do learn. Through all the horrors of human existence we learn that only love sustains, only love can be trusted, only love endures.

#48 Forgive Me My Friends

Forgive me my friends. I cannot sit beside you in your churches and your temples and pray to a far away God, in words written by strangers, from ages long since past. I must kneel beside the flowing stream and hear God/Goddess revealed in the living waters. In my darkest hour She lifted me up. She drew me near and whispered, "Do not praise me child; listen to the river that flows beneath your fears. Here we shall dance, I promise you, here we shall dance.

#49 Consolation

When you seek to console someone who is in pain, speak whatever is in your heart. Nothing that you've read will ever match the wisdom of your heart. The mind is sorely limited when these challenges arise, though it may be used as needed. If you let your heart grow wings, they will wrap around those who grieve and give them comfort, and your love will be felt at the deepest levels.

Forget the mind's doubts. Put aside its frantic counsel as to the right choice of words. Your heart will tell you when words will console and when only silence will suffice. It will let you know when you can touch another or when such touch cannot be felt. Allow the heart to rule and the mind to be the servant, and you do the will of All That Is.

#50 **Another Simple Prayer For Health**

Thank you beloved body for giving me this message. May I receive it as gracefully and painlessly as possible.

Amen.

#51 **No Turning Back**

It is not always easy to surrender to the great river of life.

The river asks that we be all of ourselves; not the fearful, small, conditioned selves whom we think we are. It is always there for us; ever flowing, ever offering us the true glory of our being. We approach it stumbling, trembling; afraid of our own magnificence. This is how it is. There is no right or wrong about it; but we can lift each other up. Those who have felt the joy of living from the current of life can offer a hand to those who are afraid – without thought of greater or less than – for it is the nature of Life to include all; to welcome, not to separate.

All of our answers can be found in the clear pure stream of our own being; for indeed it is what we are. Herein lies communion with all life, our fellow creatures, the rocks and stones that adorn our earth, the very earth itself; all part of the great river.

There is no turning back.

#52 **The Message**

When sickness is at your door, there is no doctor, no medical technique, no medication, no food, no alternative substance, which can do what getting the message your body is trying to give you can do for you. There are certainly tools that can help you greatly, by giving you the comfort level you need to calm down enough so you can get the message; but they cannot give it to you. You must fully accept it at the deepest levels of your consciousness.

Being unable to accept the message can kill you. All my medical "conditions" are the greatest gifts I have ever given to myself. Yes, in theory, I did not have to learn this way. In theory I could have gotten the message much more gently. But it was the physical symptoms which finally forced me to trust the underlying energy of my being, despite all my fears and obsessions.

Sometimes you have to be brought down to your knees, to acknowledge the God that you are.

#53 **Movement**

The act of expressing our soul in the world, when the clouds of despair engulf us, is an act of supreme faith. Not only in stillness, but in movement do we affirm what we are. Movement shakes off the webs of illusion that try to ensnare us. Through movement we reach out our hand to the Divine, and the Divine draws us unto its embrace. Through movement we summon the courage to proclaim what we are, even in the face of what we are not.

#54 **"Good and Evil"**

There is no struggle between "good and evil" raging within you; no "demons" which need to be conquered. There is only the infinite beauty of your Divine Self and the conditioned emotions which would have you deny that which you are.

That's all there ever is; truth and illusion.

It is not through waging war but through finding the courage to love yourself that you set yourself free.

#55 Our Fears

We have asked to be free and our cries have been answered. The Wave of Creation requests of us to stand, breathe deeply, and face our greatest fears. As The Wave accelerates, our fears find that they have no place to hide. They cannot go deeper into the unconscious because the Wave is stronger there now and our fears cannot tolerate the light. So they become ever more desperate because they wish to dwell in darkness, where they can control but are not seen.

Here they come now, this band of desperate mercenaries who once ruled the landscape with an iron fist, maintaining control, demanding homage. Frothing and raging, they come, displaced by an inexorable energy which is the energy of what we are, what we pray to, and what we long to be.

In truth there is nothing to fear. These mercenaries carry weapons made of mist. They only derive their power from our belief in them, and yes, they will try every trick they know to maintain that belief. But in truth they are not our mortal enemies; they are just the parts of us which have learned to hide in the darkness because we did not feel worthy of the Light.

And that my friends is the greatest of all lies, that we who are Light could ever be unworthy of Light.

#56 **Innocence**

I greet the beggar who utters outlandish phrases in the still night air. Indeed his soul may occupy realms of Grace that I can scarcely fathom. If I dared to enter such realms, might I not be propelled backwards by my own limited thoughts? When the time comes, might he sit at the right hand of God, and with infinite compassion, share his wisdom with such as I ?

This world is upside down, but purity and innocence rule the higher planes. Self righteousness breaks upon the gates of Heaven.

All are welcome, all belong. Yet first we must allow our fears and judgments, our self loathing and our rationalizations, to be burned away by the sacred fire of essence.

#57 **Birthright**

Beyond the drama and the turmoil, the ultimate wholesomeness of the universe awaits us, not as a gift but as a birthright; for indeed, it is what we are.

May we allow the river of our being to flow unfettered, to shatter the chains of disease, the spaces within us where we have forgotten our true nature. What greater act of worship is there then to express our common Divinity in human form?

#58 **Seeing**

There is no more precious gift than to truly see someone, when they do not see themselves. It is in the space of being seen that healing takes place, and the joy of life rekindled. Seeing is a gift of the heart, not of the mind, which tries to mold the "other" to meet one's expectations. It is a child of Oneness, for when we truly see someone we acknowledge that there is no other. There is only the magnificent manifestation of All That Is.

#59 To The One Who Has "Fallen Astray

The one who has "fallen astray" has not changed his sacred essence. Do you really think anyone has the power to cease to be a Divine Spark? He may have forgotten his essence, or perhaps he was rarely conscious of it during this embodiment.

Weep for him. By all means condemn his actions - but if you listen with your heart instead of your reactive mind - you will hear your heart gently weeping for the one who has forgotten who he truly is. He himself may condemn or mock you. Your own mind will leap to judge. You do not have to believe his lies, but know that beneath his lies is one thing and one thing only; fear.

Someday he will acknowledge this and your souls will embrace as old friends. Some day, perhaps, your souls will engage in the sacred joining and for that moment you will see all that he is, all that he has endured, all the ways he has hardened his heart, all the fear that he has known.

And you will take him by the hand and together you will walk through the Garden of Peace, past angels bowing silently in gratitude... and you will give thanks for the infinite chances you are given to remember who you are.

#60 Some Thoughts For These Troubled Times

Stay above the insanity as best you can, even as your heart breaks at the madness unfolding around you. You did not come here to deny the essence of your own being, to blindly obey the cultural and emotional conditioning which would have you join the chorus of hate; as desperate as that chorus may become. You were born from the great river of life; let it be your refuge, the space of your calling. For the river shall never leave you; it cannot leave you, since it is what you are.

If you wish peace, then become that for which you yearn. And when people come to you and cry, "Look sir, over there is one who would do you harm," smile and say, "Where is this other that you speak of? I see only one who is the same as I. I see but my Divine Self looking out through different eyes."

#61 The Silence Of Trees

If you wish to kill yourselves over your beliefs please leave me out of it.

I will be walking on a country road, overcome by the silence of trees.

#62 Creativity

The soul longs to create, but as with every human endeavor, this longing becomes entwined with our sense of incompleteness. We wonder if we are good enough, if the fruits of our creation will be accepted, or if they will be greeted by deafening indifference or mockery. All of our wounds, barely conscious, whisper our perceived inadequacies, encrusting the dazzling jewel from which our creative expression emerges. Perhaps we still harbor the dream that our creativity will help us to survive in the physical world, attracting the resources which we so desperately need.

The soul longs to create, and that desire is an eternal expression of our Divinity within the great river of life. As with all aspects of the human condition (relationships, knowledge, physical desires); fulfillment does not come from repressing, but from releasing the sense of incompleteness which underlies, distorts and attempts to control. As we remember what we are, our creative expressions become simple acts of sharing, in harmony with the Divine love that is our essential nature.

Magically we discover that when we give up the need to be heard, people begin to hear us.

#63 **The Future**

Experiencing your magnificence, moving into the future that your soul longs for, can at times be terrifying . This is because on many levels we have made peace with our perceived limitations. We have defined our relationships, accepted our "shortcomings", lived with our illnesses, embraced the joys we have managed to wean from life; all on the basis of our existing consciousness. We know that there must be something more, but when consciousness begins to shift. and the soul begins to stir, our minds react with fear. "Things may not be great," whispers the mind, "but what if I lose everything I have?"

To be true to our calling we must stand in the unknown, breathe into our desperation, and simply do what is in front of us to do as best we can. Emotionally we might feel like the winds of change are tearing us apart, but when the storm subsides, we find ourselves standing next to whatever our heart desires.

As it says on page one of A Course In Miracles: "Nothing real can be threatened. Nothing unreal exists. Herein lies the peace of God."

A very good adage to remember. Especially in times like these.

#64 Peace

I know this world is rife with horror. The mighty shake off the lowly like dust from their shoes. "How dare you feel peace?" my troubled mind rebukes me.

I stand on the earth in its cloak of freshly fallen snow, overwhelmed by the pulsating stillness. The chill air caresses me like a lover.

"How can I not," I answer through tears. "How can I not?"

#65 Your Ego

It never ceases to amaze me how close your ego can come to destroying you in its endless quest to keep you safe!

#66 The Doctor's Confession

I have given your symptoms a name. I am not aware of the grave disservice which I have just done by doing so because no one ever taught me differently. If fact, all of my training has been about giving names to your "conditions" - quantifying them, objectifying them - removing them from the sphere of your own creative consciousness.

What I name, in all its terror and hopelessness, becomes your reality. But the worst crime is that I have not walked with you into the spaces in which you gave birth to your symptoms, because, in truth, I do not know how. With all of my training, all of my degrees, all of my investment; I have no idea what battles you are waging against your own being that have brought you to my door.

No idea whatsoever.

So I am left to devoting my considerable talents to manipulating your physical reality. This is no small matter, and indeed, my colleagues and I have achieved extraordinary successes in this regard, which we have every right to be proud of. Yet for all of the remarkable contributions which we have made in alleviating human suffering, I cannot help you to heal yourself. I cannot help you because I do not see you. I do not see what your soul is striving to achieve, and the ways in which your fear is desperately fighting against you.

If I could see you than I would also see that your physical symptoms are the ultimate manifestation of this battle. And I could help point the way to your liberation. The choice would always remain yours, but at least I could point the way. And so you, my patient, are left on your own. You may pick and choose from what I have to offer, but please do not surrender to me if I ask you to. It will be tempting because you are afraid, but deep inside you know it would be a violation of your own being.

.

#67 All Is Well

The great cosmic winds disintegrate the man I thought I was. The once mighty constructs of my ego are strewn about like patio furniture in a hurricane.

All is well.

Unspeakable fears rush in to fill the empty spaces. Images of horror assail me. The mind howls in desperate cries of judgment and survival.

All is well

About me my fellow men denounce each other in increasingly shrill tones; their upraised voices ascend to the rafters, shaking the human edifice.

All is well.
I surrender to the great winds of Creation.

They whisper in my heart that we are One.

With profound gratitude I receive the gift of life.

#68 Return To Love

Surround yourself with people who have committed themselves to being the love that is All That Is. Do not expect them to never be seduced by fear, for fear seduces even the strongest among us. Ask only that they return to love. Surround yourself with people who have made the commitment to return to love, and together you will build a new world.

It doesn't matter what they believe, what books they have read, or what status they have achieved in this world of dreams. It matters only that they have chosen to be who they truly are.

#69 Embracing

When we stop recoiling from what we don't want to look at - when we open our arms, breathe deeply, and embrace those aspects of ourselves which we have become separated from - we find there is a radiant being looking back at us each morning in the mirror; and that is who we are.

#70 Fear

No one can not give in to fear for you.

You have to do that yourself.

You can stand before the greatest Master,

And still you have do that for yourself.

For many of us,

That's the hardest part.

#71 **More Reflections On Love**

Nothing is impossible with Love. Love shatters the rotting bonds of logic. It defies all conventions. It never separates, for all are included in its sacred circle. Only fear –the mortal enemy of love - can separate; but never love.

When love graces your life, allow it dominion. Treasure it. Do not resist, but do not force it cithcr. Love possesses its own rhythm, unfolding as it does in Divine order. All who encounter love are blessed by love. Love uplifts the old and the worn, and makes the angels laugh in delight. It rekindles long abandoned dreams.

I bow to love. I kiss the feet of love.

Forever, it shall be my Master.

#72 **As Creation, What's Next**

A tremendous energy shift is going on as I type these words. A wave of profound peace has descended upon the stillness between my thoughts. This is the playground of the soul, where time dissolves and nothing exists except being.

Here there is no "right" or "wrong". Here there are no desperate voices pleading to be heard. Here the stillness beckons, calling you forth.

"As Creation, What's next?" the wise ones once told me. "Let this be your mantra upon awakening each morning."
"As Creation, What's next?" I inquire.

No words.

Just abiding sacredness,

And peace

#73 **Your Thoughts**

One day you realize that the thoughts which make you miserable, as seductive as they appear, are like spider webs dancing in the wind. On this day you lay claim to the mastery of your consciousness. On this day, you cease to be the terrified prey of your own ethereal creations, and you exercise your Divine right to express your soul authentically in the world.

Your terrifying thoughts return to the mist from which they were born. You have set them free, free to transform themselves into a higher and purer expression of All That Is.

#74 **Surrender**

The shift is palpable now. The moorings have been torn apart and scattered to the winds. What has been unassembled cannot be made whole. Our bindings served us well, but now it is the hour of our calling; the moment when the soul's dreams are given birth into form.

Yesterday's harbors have turned to mist. Turn and look for them if you must, but in your heart you know that they are gone. Now, there is only the deep, unending current of the river; carrying within it the yearning and the design of your soul.

The mind craves the old warmth of the campfire; it plays in the shadows and makes the dying embers seem alive. But the ashes have been scattered and there is no warmth in these shadows anymore. There will be new campfires, new celebrations, new adventures; but first you must surrender everything to the great river of life.

#75 **How You Feel**

It's not always about how you feel.

It's about remembering who you are

Regardless of how you feel.

This is the supreme teacher.

This is the meaning of faith.

#76 **Fear At The Gates**

Sometimes you are stripped of everything but your own Divinity. Fear howls at the gates of your consciousness, threatening to devour all that you think you are. You are powerless, too weary to resist.

At these moments, if you but summon the courage to surrender, the Wave of Creation will lift you up. Like a mountain stream it will flow through you; and fear will bow and dissolve into mist.

#77 Re-membering

So many of our struggles would cease if we could just believe in our own deep purity, as aspects of a Creative force, regardless of what we might be experiencing.

Our thoughts are like storm clouds that appear to hide the sun.

Yet the sun is not extinguished by the clouds, and the majesty of Creation is not extinguished by fleeting thoughts. It is what we are.

#78 The Source

At age 65 my life is just beginning. A force courses through me, fueled by a cosmic generator that my mind cannot fathom. All my thoughts and emotions are a pale reflection of this Divine energy which vibrates beneath the person that I once thought I was. It knows nothing of age or infirmity, for it exists beyond time or disease. It twirls about and dances with abandon, yet there is a purpose to its movement.

I am compelled by the sacred river of life. Even when I refuse to align with it; I am compelled by it. I exist! I AM! I wish to climb the highest mountaintop and proclaim this truth to all.

#79 God

If you are looking for God, close your eyes and allow all of your thoughts, emotions, and physical sensations to pass through you.

What is left is the Essence of God.

#80 Feeling Safe

It is far too great a burden to place on the shoulders of another to make them responsible for you feeling safe in the Universe.

#81 So What?

Two of the most important words in the English language are "so what?". Apply them at the end of your judgments (especially about others) and you will have grasped one of the most profound spiritual principles you will ever encounter.

#82 My Peace

You ask how I can be joyful or at peace while so many horrors are unfolding in this world? I answer, "How can I argue with my own being?"

To deny peace, to deny joy, is to deny my very essence. As much as my mind would have me do this, as much as my ego would cry, "All is lost," I cannot embrace these delusions. No, I will allow such lies to be swallowed up by the Divine river and smashed against the rocks.

I will not allow humanity's resistance to its own Divinity, and the ensuing chaos, make me deny the truth of my being. I know that the destruction, born of the refusal to accept the accelerating Light, will end; but the Light will continue and prevail.

Humanity is learning to embrace its own being.

My heart dances to the current of the great river of life.

#83 Easter Blessing

Bless the darkness within you and bring the sweetness of the Universal Christ - which is your essence - to envelop that darkness and become resurrected. Cast off the deathly shadow of fear, and proclaim, once and for all, that you are a perfect expression of All That Is. Then become a true disciple of Christ - not through any belief system or religion - but through the expression of your Divine soul in the world.

#84 The Other Internet

There is another Internet, far more powerful than the one we are familiar with. It is the "Internet" of energy which weaves through all life, and flows through every soul. All we need to do to align with this energy is to dare to express who we truly are.

We can't control this river of life with our minds. Our egos will always obsess about "outcome" and "survival". If we can let all of this go and surrender, we will find there are a million outstretched hands waiting to uplift us, and to help us navigate the waters. These are the hands of our brothers and sisters, seen and unseen.

Please don't focus on what is falling apart. Focus instead on what you have to share, for it is needed now more than ever.

#85 The Call Of The Mother

The Mother is finally receiving Her due. No longer is she content to remain hidden in deep forest caves with her ways honored in darkness. Many now hear her call - not in opposition to the Father - but in full balance and respect. The way of the heart, of the nurturer, of the soft green moss, of the sweet rainfall on the forest floor, of the newborn calf, of the mourner's cry, of those who have been silent, of those who heal, of the mother and babe and the old man on the brink of death.

Without the Feminine rising, the Masculine would destroy everything it has built. Alone, it lacks the wisdom to sustain itself and its creations. All around us the temples of the mind are crumbling. Can you not hear the cold stones as they crash upon the earth? The Mother flows through the desolation, nurturing her earth with the greatest compassion, as new forms emerge that serve life, and balance is restored between heart and mind.

#86 **Don't Be Afraid**

Don't be afraid.

The same accelerating energy which, when resisted, causes people to tear each other apart, will bring you the fulfillment of everything your soul longs for.

You can ride this wave!

Open your heart to those who cling desperately to their fears; but drink deeply from the river of life which is flowing faster now than it ever has.

Despite what it looks like, the part of you that remembers rejoices.

#87 **Sanity And Insanity**

The difference between sanity and insanity lies in whether you acknowledge and observe your thoughts; or whether you believe them.

#88 What Am I?

What am I? I am a vibrating Creative Force. I am a particle of God expressing through the disguise of a man. This is not a quaint New Age belief. Nor is it some notion that I came up with by studiously reading metaphysical writings. This is what I experience. If I sit still for even a moment and close my eyes; this is what I experience! And it is getting stronger. It is getting stronger by the day. I don't have to sing hymns of praise to the Divine. All I have to do is close my eyes and the Divine embraces me. Indeed, it embraces me as what I am.

In the space of no-thought dwells the primordial energy of Creation. It is felt most intensely behind my eyes, but I am learning to bring it down through the central channel of my body because this is where it needs to go. When I become afraid, I block its flow and suffer. But - while my fears may make me temporarily uncomfortable - they can never damn this river.

This experience brings with it a certain responsibility. As always, the responsibility is primarily to myself, and then to others. The responsibility is to honor myself enough to be true to the current of my own life force. Nothing, absolutely nothing, is more important than this. Whatever desires I have should not be suppressed, but they should not be my primary focus either. Focusing on the things I think I need is like stepping off the train and sitting at the bench at the station thinking about how I intend to get to the next stop!

The River of Life brings everything my human self authentically needs, and in ways I never dreamed possible. All I have to do is to honor its flow.

And the flow of the River has but one desire; to serve the whole.

#89 **You Are Creation**

To consciously experience the Wave of Creation - especially now as it accelerates so profoundly - is to experience a flood of energy cascading into your consciousness-vibrating, bursting with a myriad images -transforming the limited self from its belief systems, its neediness, its diseases, and its grip of death. This is not philosophy. This is not an idea entertained with your mind. This is earth shattering transformation that tears apart the latticework of your limitations from head to toe, exploding the deepest emotional patterns that you have constructed over a lifetime to keep you safe, exposing the codependency in your relationships, laying you bare to your own deepest dreams. All that you can do is realize that you **are** Creation, and then observe your dying "self", without judgment, from the perspective of the surging current of your Divinity. It is here, in the great river of life, that all prayers are answered, not in the plaintive pleas to a God outside of you. It is here that your soul gives birth to its glorious expression in the world.

#90 **Psalm 23 Interpreted**

The Lord is my shepherd; I shall not want.

Divinity - the infinite Force which I Am - protects me in my humanness. My ego is like a little sheep in the vastness of the Creative Force which guides me in this human existence. As I open to this Force, all of my needs are met. I want for nothing.

He maketh me to lie down in green pastures: he leadeth me beside the still waters.

As I learn to open to this Divine Energy and allow it to flow through me, the rocky roads and the pain give way to flowering fields and joy. The turbulence and the chaos yield to still waters where I can nurture and refresh my spirit.

He restoreth my soul: he leadeth me in the paths of righteousness for his name's sake.

Divine Energy moving through me makes me aware of my soul's true purpose, that which I designed before coming into this body. As I learn to feel the calling of my soul, I manifest "righteousness," because this is the deepest expression of my essence. I exist "for his name's sake": for the Source which is constantly fulfilling itself through me.

Yea, though I walk through the valley of the shadow of death, I will fear no evil: for thou art with me; thy rod and thy staff they comfort me.

At birth I enter the "valley of the shadow of death". This illusory shadow hangs over my human existence. Aligned with the God within, there is nothing to fear from the horrors that I can be subjected to. The Energy is with me always, for it is who I Am. It cannot abandon me. I can lean on the bliss of Creative Energy; it serves as my rod and my staff during the challenging times of my human existence.

Thou preparest a table before me in the presence of mine enemies: thou anointest my head with oil; my cup runneth over.

Truly I have no enemies when I am aligned with All That Is. The feast is the direct experience of Divinity; even in the face of those who would wish to do me harm. It is always there, beneath the fear. Through aligning with the Grace of this Energy, I am anointed and blessed with abundance.

*Surely goodness and mercy shall follow me all the days of my life:
and I will dwell in the house of the Lord forever.*

All that I will ever need for the expression of my soul's purpose
flows to me as I live from the Divine energy which I Am. In death
I continue to blossom in the magnificent abode of the One.

#91 Ode To The River

My words break upon the rocks like mist
Dissolving into the great river of life

I am intoxicated with Creation
With the current of my own being

I bow in gratitude
To All That Is

The gratitude becomes a mighty wave
That cleanses me of all human sorrows
In how many lives have I longed for this?
In what desolate places have I worshipped you?

What sufferings did I bear
Only to come to the realization

That you were as real
As my very next breath

Now that I know,
I will never desert you again

For you are the wellspring
The boundless Source of my life

The giver of gifts

The healer of wounds

You have birthed and nurtured me
Since before time

Only you exist
Experiencing through the illusion of 'I"

I rejoice in this illusion
That we have created together

Until I merge fully unto you
Into the everlasting bliss of Creation

#92 **The Poem**

My life is an ever expanding poem.
I make up the verses
As I go along.

It doesn't matter what happened
"Back then"
In a place bounded by a time
That never existed

My only "time" is now
I am on fire with now
Wont you join me in this dance?

Holding hands
Swirling together
In the Divine Circle
Beyond all needs

Beyond the shriveled beings
We once thought we were
We laugh as we hear our chains
Clanging to the ground

We laugh in reverence
To each other
To All That Is
To All That Ever Was

Eternal Grace
Flowing in endless harmony
That we are a part of
That is what we are

#93 **The Embrace**

Wounded people touching
Their souls embrace
Dispelling the illusion of teacher student
And all such lies

Bearing witness
In honor and in awe
Beyond all conceptions of what love is
Beyond all ordained roles

In searing honesty
Beyond all perceived needs
Daring to reveal
The beauty and the terror of being

Their God Selves wrap around each other
In a place where mind dares not enter
In a place that has banished fear
In an Eternal Dance

"You may be you"
They whisper
And the words echo off a million stars

"We need nothing."

"We are free".

II. STORIES

#94 **The Twelve Roses Of The Cross**

This morning I woke up and Jesus was with me. Now that is strange since I am not a Christian (born again or otherwise). But there he was - projection, thought form, Son Of God - you decide.

I asked him what he thought of my latest idea; "The Twelve Roses of the Cross". We would create a garden with twelve beautiful rose bushes; each a different color to symbolize a particular aspect of Mastery. There would be a pink rose bush for Self Love (the very first), a yellow rose bush for Forgiveness, a white rose bush for Purity; you get the idea. The last rose bush would be purple for Compassion and alignment with the Divine.

At each bush people would stop, open their hearts, and meditate on the message. The good news is Jesus would be waiting at the end of the garden, to put his arms around each person, and give them a big hug.

Between you and me, he really liked the idea! He felt it was a lot more appropriate than having people work themselves into a frenzy about crucifixion, blood and those kinds of things.

Especially the children; he wants so bad that we not expose the children to that stuff. If we feel we need to do this, he wont interfere, but honestly, it breaks his heart.

We talked a little about how to publicize our new endeavor and we decided we better keep a low profile. He was particularly concerned that The Twelve Roses of the Cross not become the foundation of a new religion that forced its adherents to circumambulate the garden. He told me the last thing he wanted was for the children to be forced to put on stiff clothes and stare somberly at the rose bushes while some guy in black intoned his name!

But you should have seen the smile on his face when he envisioned each of us finally making it to that last bush! I don't think there is a greater gift which anybody could possibly give him - no cathedral, no Hallelujah Chorus, no fundraiser - nothing even close.

And all this before my morning coffee.

I hope He comes back tomorrow.

#95 **A Miracle At The Supermarket**

Today I experienced a miracle at the supermarket.

It all started out simply enough. A woman was standing next to me and I thought I perceived some sadness in her. I got the impression to send peace and joy to her solar plexus, the area which is often called the "seat of the soul." She didn't know it, but I was trying to bolster her energy field.

Within minutes I began to witness one of the most spectacular transformations I have even seen.

No, there was no visible change in the woman standing next to me. She didn't light up, skip or dance. She didn't turn around and say, "Oh my God, I feel some great power emanating from you, sir. Who are you?"

Nothing even remotely like that.

The miracle that I am referring to occurred within me. I felt a sudden outpouring of compassion; a genuine, abiding respect and love for this woman whom I had never even met! I was taken aback by the intensity of my love toward a total stranger. The feeling welled up and came through me like a great wave. I kept saying to myself, "Wow, this must be a glimpse of what we really are, before the earthly conditioning sets in." Even now, when I think about it, I almost cry.
Yes, it was a truly miraculous day.

#96 **The Stranger In The Coffee Shop**

My mother would often pour out her heart to total strangers.

My family owned a fruit and vegetable stand, and Ma would regularly regale the customers with the major existential dilemmas of her life (which usually included me). Years later, when I would come to town, I'd inevitably meet somebody for the first time and they would look at me oddly and remark, "Aren't you the guy who dropped out of Yale to join a commune?"

"Yeah, I'm the guy."

One day I was eating at Pluto's, the fast food joint across from our house. A man with a worn face sat down next to me. He stared at me for a few moments, then asked, "Aren't you Ted Slipchinsky?" I swallowed the last bite of my fake lobster salad sandwich and warily replied, "Yes, that's me."

With barely concealed rage, the man launched into a long tirade. I was shocked at his words, doled out to a total stranger on a stool in a fast food restaurant.

But to this man I was no stranger. "It makes me sick," he sputtered, his eyes penetrating through my defenses into the fortress of my soul. He shook his head, like a judge passing sentence. "It makes me sick when I think that someone would throw away an opportunity that so many people would die for. One of the finest institutions in the world, only one year left, and you spit in its face." The man paused and drew his breath. "Threw it in the garbage, for what?" He paused again and looked at me in utter disdain. "To go live with a bunch of hippies."

Sometimes you get startled so badly your well worn defenses are useless. At these times, if you listen deeply, you may hear the voice of your heart. I looked into the man's eyes, but instead of anger, all I could perceive was the sadness of a million lost dreams. From somewhere beyond my mind the words appeared.

"Did something like this happen to you?" I asked, surprised by the gentleness of my own voice.

The man looked at me in disbelief. Then his face softened and his eyes grew moist. "Yes, something happened to me, he sighed, and put down his coffee cup. "The Depression happened to me, and to a million others just like me."

He took a deep breath and began to speak. He told me how he had wanted to be a doctor since he was ten, had worked after school and saved his money; how his farmer parents had struggled to help him, how he had gotten accepted into one of the best medical schools in the country, and finally, how he had to drop out of school to save the family farm." It was a familiar story, told a thousand times in a thousand sad voices.

Then the man got up and slowly shook my hand.

"I wish you well" he said kindly. "I hope things work out better for you than they did for me."

#97 A Love Story

Many years ago I was having dinner alone at a restaurant somewhere in CT. I was sitting in a booth with a large partition between it and the next booth over.

After I ordered my meal, I could not help but overhear a conversation coming from the booth behind the partition. I heard an old man's voice, speaking in a thick Yiddish accent, in a tone that one would use when addressing a young child. I don't remember his exact words, but I recall that he was helping the child order dinner.

"Now what would you like dear", he said very sweetly (or something to that effect). How about the tuna salad? You always liked tuna salad. Do you think you want that? And what should we get you to drink, honey. Would you like some skim milk, or maybe a diet cola?"

The old man continued to speak ever so gently. I assumed that the child was too young to talk, because he or she remained silent. Then I heard the footsteps of the waitress behind me, and I heard the old man state his order. I don't recall what he said, but I noticed that his voice became dignified, almost formal. I remarked to myself that this seemed a little odd, and then I forgot about it.

After I paid the waitress, I stood up, and walked by the table where the old man had, I assumed, been taking his grandchild out to dinner. Suddenly he lifted his head, his eyes caught mine, and he looked directly into my soul. He appeared to be in his eighties, slightly hunched with only a shock of white hair, and deep piercing eyes. He was in the act of feeding soup across the table to a frail elderly woman, about his age, who had a vacant look, and was clearly suffering from dementia. All he said was, "Fifty years. Fifty wonderful years. And now this. What can I do?"

I looked at him and tried to respond but my eyes filled with tears and I could not think of any words. These were not the "beautiful people" whose images we are constantly being bombarded with from the media. They were old and frail and life had clearly taken

its toll on them. But as I headed for the parking lot, I silently
thanked them for teaching me the meaning of love.

#98 **The Old Man And The Young Woman**

The young woman looked at the old man tottering toward her, bent
so low he could scarcely see above the cobblestones at his feet.
With each step his ghostly frame shook and his drawn face
contorted in pain. "How sad", the young woman thought, "how
terribly sad that any human must suffer so."

She slowed her step, earnestly hoping that the old man would turn
off into one of the simple cottages that lined the well worn road. In
truth, she was afraid, disturbed by the horrible suffering that the
old man represented. She wished desperately that this suffering
would not take up residence in her pristine world.

Slowly, inexorably, like a living nightmare, the old man stumbled
forward, edging closer to her slight frame, until she could have
reached out and touched his hand.

Then something deep inside her caused the young woman to turn
her head to look at the old man's face. Her mind resisted, but an
irresistible force drew her eyes toward his. When she met his gaze,
a radiance beyond measure burst forth from the old man's eyes,
and a love so pure that the young woman lost all sense of time and
space, and fell trembling to the ground. Lips quivering, filled with
incredible ecstasy, she dropped to her knees, under the spell of the
old man.

"Forgive me Lord," she murmured. "Forgive me for being so
deceived by form that I could ever deny your eternal radiance."
The old man smiled. A thousand stars were kindled in some far off
heaven. "There is nothing to forgive," child, he whispered, as he

reached down to take her arm. "From this moment you will remember to see the Divine even in the lowliest among you; for this is my essence, theirs and yours."

#99 Message From A Man's Heart

Around five years ago I underwent two coronary angioplasties. Two stents were put in a coronary artery that had three blockages; one 99 percent, one 90 percent and one 75 percent. On day two the same procedure was applied to a second artery that had a 75 percent blockage. Lesser blockages remained, but these were not deemed bad enough to do anything about.

The truth is my heart was being slowly deprived of nourishment (blood and oxygen) for years. As I reflected on all this after the procedures, it became clear that this condition was a physical manifestation of the fact that I was not nurturing my heart in my daily life. I was, all too often, unresponsive to its calls. My fears were obscuring its voice, so its voice became a cry, and this cry eventually forced me to act; possibly saving my physical life.

Two days after I got out of the hospital, I had an interesting experience. As I was sitting at a table in a coffee shop near my house, an African American man who appeared to be around 55 years old sat down a few tables away from me. Our eyes met and we nodded. He was carrying two flat styrofoam containers. I was all too familiar with the type of food usually found in these containers at this establishment, and I assumed that it was probably fried or fatty.

Suddenly I got the impression to joke with this man I didn't know about my recent cardiac "adventures", and to mention the dangers of eating fatty foods. In response, my mind went into "protection" mode ("you're crazy, you're going to offend this man, you'll make an ass of yourself, you don't even know the guy", etc, etc). Something inside me, however, pushed me to override my mind's habitual "safeguards" and I blurted out, "Gotta watch those fatty foods; I just had three stents put in my arteries".

The man turned his head and stared. For a second I thought the habitual "protector" was right. Then he began asking me a series of questions: "how old was I, what physical condition was I in, what cardiac procedures had been done to me?" etc.
Within minutes, he poured out his story. He was a truck driver and he had suffered a heart attack at age 48. His truck had been parked at a stoplight and a nurse who pulled up next to him observed him going into cardiac arrest. He was rushed to a nearby trauma center and fortunately his heart did not suffer any significant damage.

Then this man, whom moments earlier I was afraid to address, looked at me and said, "I think you're an angel". I laughed out loud. He said "my father was a pastor and he taught me that everything happens for a reason. I think maybe God sent you to have this conversation with me".

We laughed together about this theological possibility. I asked him how he was doing since his heart attack. He said that, with the pressures of work, his diet had deteriorated badly. (He gestured to two large slices of pizza in the styrofoam containers on the table in front of him). I asked him if still gets chest pains and, somewhat sheepishly, he replied, "occasionally". When we parted he kept thanking me over and over and saying "God bless you". I felt like I had just made a life long friend. Then I realized the residual soreness I had felt from my own procedures had evaporated during our 20 minute conversation.

These days I take many more such "risks" and they have been working out just fine. So now I am going to take another one, and suggest that you take the time each day to listen to your heart; and to heed its calls. If you think this sounds like an advertising jingle I won't be offended. Something still beating inside me wants to give you this message.

#100 Caution To The Wind And A Bag Of Fritos

Today I threw caution to the wind and ate an entire bag of Fritos, while resting my backside against the trunk of my old Honda Accord. No, it was not that big bag you might be conjuring up in your mind, but a medium sized one (only around ten servings, I suppose). Still the sodium and caloric content would send any dedicated cardiologist (including my own) into cardiac arrest.

Some would call my Frito eating frenzy the manifestation of a death wish. I prefer to think of it as an affirmation of life. It felt good, and I was thumbing my nose at all those wonderful medical authorities (usually under 40 years old with ridiculously flat stomachs) who mean well and do good work but who, let's face it, often don't have a clue. Don't get me wrong; they are nice people. It seems however that far too often they are prisoners of their own models.

I am fine. Perhaps I will get one of those 30 foot banners with the big red letters made up and drape it across the front of my log cabin: "TED IS FINE!" it shall proclaim to the world beyond my front yard (a world of pickup trucks, deer hunters, vegans, old timers and city transplants; all living in something close to harmony). God/Goddess has never left me. She reverberates through my being with every breath I am blessed to take. A youth might see a man in the "final" quarter of his life. I see a man who is finally getting out of his way enough to express his soul in the world. Such expression is the fountain of youth, my friends; a vibrating, flowing river of endless life.

We will all know it soon enough when we touch the spaces that our near death experiencer friends have. But, as they always seem to tell us, the real trick is to touch those spaces now, as best we can, in these bodies; and discover that we never really left them.

Joy to you all from my heart to yours; and solace for all our sufferings.

#101 **The Blessings Of The Roses**

A few years ago, I went to see some friends in a spiritual group that I was involved in. We were sitting outside at a picnic table, and some of the women started paying attention to me, in a sweet, innocently flirtatious way.

Suddenly something opened in my heart. It was a deeply physical sensation which is difficult to describe. But then, as was often the case, I distracted myself with fear.

Something about the deep heart opening that I had experienced - and the abrupt sense of fear which closed it down - had a severe physical impact on my body. It was not a sharp pain, but a very pronounced sense that my heart was being "muffled"; as if the lid of a frying pan were being clamped down on it. Physically I became very weak. I was undergoing a very uncomfortable and intense process which would not shut off. I felt like if it continued this way, it was going to kill me. I went home and lied down on the couch and only told one friend about it.

All I could do was lie there and feel my wounded, muffled heart, seemingly getting worse. It was as if my heart could not tolerate having opened so much and then closing so abruptly through fear. It seemed to be telling me, "if this is the way you choose to be, this is how I must react. I can't take this anymore."

I lay on the couch, refusing to see a doctor, feeling weaker and weaker; thinking to myself "you really did it this time". This went on for at least two days. Finally, from somewhere deep inside of me, I got an impression to say one sentence, and to say it three times. Not really knowing why, I found myself saying, "I open my heart to give and to receive love fully. I open my heart to give and to receive love fully. I open my heart to give and to receive love fully." After the third time, I knew that I would recover, and that the intense process that was wearing me down had come to an end.

I was still extremely weak and I couldn't take the slightest negativity. I couldn't even talk to the mailman. Then somehow I was guided to go to the place of my healing. It was not a cardiology department. It was not a famous doctor. It was an outdoor rose garden in a neighboring city that was open to the public.

At first I was too weak to go for more than a half hour. Gradually I increased the time I spent at the rose garden. I would linger next to each beautiful bush, and I could feel the healing energy restoring my heart. To this day I am convinced that no modern medicine could have brought me back to life and mended my wounded heart the way those beloved rose bushes did.

This is my tale of surrender and returning to self love.

May you receive the blessings of the roses, today and forever.

#102 The Two Paths

One day an old man, wracked with pain, shuffled down a road until he came to a certain fork. On the one side was a narrow path, ancient but mostly hidden from view by tall grasses. On the other side was a much broader path, which had clearly seen far more use. In fact, the old man could make out many travelers on this second path, grim and determined, plodding along, refusing to look up or about, as if the path itself held them in some kind of spell.

For a long time the old man paused at the crossroads, pondering the meaning of the scene which was unfolding before him. He too could feel the powerful seduction of the broader path, and he could feel a deep emotion, which had lay partially buried within him since childhood, to allow it to pull him onto it.

But the old man was no fool. So he stood on the earth, feet firmly planted on the ground, and called upon his heart to help him to understand the meaning of the two paths. After some time, he received his answer.

"There are two paths," his heart spoke, with great gentleness, "the path of gratitude and the path of bitterness. Those who are ruled by their fears will choose the second path, for the voice of fear can drown out all other voices. Its offer of anger and bitterness, as the antidote to pain, will seduce many. But for those who believe in their true self, in the magnificence which lies beyond fear, the path of gratitude will always be revealed to them as the wisest choice."

The old man felt a sparkling, loving energy move up and down his body. He knew that the One, the unfathomable One of which he was a part, would love him with a love beyond human understanding, no matter which path he took. He knew the One would always see through his fear into the perfection which lie at his core. But he heeded his heart and stepped forward and placed his foot firmly on the ancient path of gratitude.

Suddenly the seemingly barren, hidden path burst into bloom. Oceans of resplendent wildflowers revealed themselves on both sides. Sunlight burst through the trees and illumined it with a Divine glow. The old man understood, without a whisper of self-judgment, how he had created his own pain; but because he chose the path of acceptance and gratitude, every step he took brought him healing.

At long last he remembered who he was; a being of Light manifesting love.

III. TEACHINGS

#103 **Transformation**

It was over forty years ago that I first felt the existence of a profound spiritual energy. How inexact these words "spiritual energy" are; symbols of the prison that language ensnares us in.

There was nothing subtle about this great power. It arrived like a whirlwind and I knew immediately that it was different from anything my consciousness had ever experienced. This was not emotion, not physical sensation, not the mental thoughts that obsessed me; indeed, it was the very foundation from which all thought and emotion arose. It was as if the spaces between my thoughts, the stillness, had come to life as a vibrating, pulsating force. I soon realized that if I did whatever was in front of me to do, in the way that I believed was highest and best, I would feel a oneness with this energy that was coursing through me. On the other hand, if I became afraid, and let my mind take me, the energy would become blocked and I would become befuddled and lost, spiraling downward.

This energy refashions consciousness like a potter refashions clay. For many years, I lost touch with it, but it never left me. For many years I tried to live "normally", but I failed. Than one day, around 20 years ago, while reading some accounts of near death experiences, something reawakened deep within me. A familiarity, a knowing was rekindled. "I am not crazy", I told myself. "The energy is real". At that moment I threw a switch deep within myself and gave myself permission to experience the incredible power of this force once again. I asked the universe to help me feel dynamic and the force came roaring back like a pride of lions; lions of love, lions of fierce beauty and oneness.

I will never again consciously abandon this Energy. It is the unfolding of my soul. It is the Grace through which I remember and create myself. I bow to it. It lifts me up. I would gladly bow to it for all eternity, but it whispers with the deepest compassion, "Don't you have things to do, my son?"

It's smile lights the galaxies with a radiance beyond measure.

#104 **How To Deal With Fear**

I would like to speak about fear. It is a subject I am quite familiar with, having done extensive "field work" in the area (that is to say, having experienced a great deal of anxiety over the years). During this time I have managed to learn a few things and I would like to share some of them here.

Most of us know by now that resisting, denying or nurturing fear only serves to magnify it; that the most effective way to deal with fear is to acknowledge it, breathe into it, and let it go. I wholeheartedly agree with this assessment.

There is something else that I have discovered about fear which I feel is sometimes overlooked. This discovery has been a cornerstone of my life. What I have discovered is that fear will completely lose its grip, that it will utterly dissolve, once I give myself permission, at the deepest level of my being, to release it. By "giving myself permission" I mean that I truly decide, at all levels, that my fear is not justified; that it is a distortion of my genuine experience of the moment.

For example, suppose one day you get a call from your doctor who somberly informs you that your x-ray is "suspicious". Being human, you will undoubtedly experience a wave of fear, and it will not be easy to let go of it. If the next day the doctor calls you back and says, "I'm terribly sorry, we totally misread your x-ray and it is completely normal"; your fear will be lifted off you very dramatically. The difference between your first response and your second is that, in the first case, your deepest emotions are telling you that fear is a justified response to your situation. In the second scenario (after the misdiagnosis is revealed) these same emotions tell you that your fear is no longer valid, that you no longer have anything to be afraid of. So what happened in this second scenario? After all is said and done, you gave yourself permission to let go of fear. You decided that your fear was not justified by your circumstances; that it would be inauthentic, even delusional to feel fear when there was no longer any valid reason to.

We may not necessarily face this dramatic a situation when we encounter fears in our lives. I would submit, however, that when we experience fear for whatever reason, on some level we are giving ourselves permission to feel it, because we believe it is "justified" or worthy of putting energy into. We may tell ourselves on a mental level that we are turning everything over to God, or that we just need to let the fear go-but the crux of the matter is that the fear will never really dissolve until we believe, deep inside, that it is unjustified and illusory-that is to say, until we give ourselves permission to release it.

There is one more amazing thing I have learned. I have learned that as soon as I truly make the inner decision that my fear is an illusion; it dissolves almost instantly. In fact it dissolves in direct proportion to the extent that I have decided it is unreal. Time and time again, fears that have paralyzed me and seemed momentous turn to mist, the minute I throw that inner switch; the minute I decide that the energy associated with the fear is a distortion, that the fear itself is simply not real. (At this point someone usually says, "well what if you are being attacked by a Grizzly bear"? Fine, I'll give you that one. But the bears in my neighborhood are brown bears; very shy and almost always harmless).

I was once told by some wise channeled friends that "any fear let go of in faith shall manifest for the highest good". In other words, anything I am afraid of will be taken care of and will work out for the best, if I simply let the fear go and focus on the moment I am in. Do you realize what a completely liberating statement that is? It is one of the most liberating statements you will ever hear!

Moreover, the principle has proven itself to me, down to the tiniest detail, time and time again. If I had managed to believe it consistently I would have saved myself a great deal of emotional grief and physical illness over the years.

But I am getting much better at this game. I am beginning to see the alchemy revealed when I finally give myself permission to live my life fearlessly. I am finally allowing myself to simply be.

I highly recommend this for us all.

#105 **Allowing Your Divinity To Flow**

You will not find God in some far off Heaven or in the abstract edifices of your mind. You will find God in your own body; the very last place you may think to look. It is quite simple really. To experience the Creation which you are a part of, you need to allow this force to flow freely through the vessel of your humanness.

There is no other way. You will always remain a spark of All That Is, whether the Divine Energy is blocked or flowing; but to consciously experience it - to feel the joy, purposefulness, vibrancy, health and clarity which It offers - this Energy cannot be withheld from the physical structure that you are functioning through. It may seem like a cosmic joke; that the profound truths you are looking for, are only revealed to you when you bring the Wave of Creation down from the top of your head, to your root, and then into the earth. Yet this is how it is.

It is your deeply rooted emotional patterns, and the intellectual justifications you provide for them with your belief systems, which keep your energy congealed. Then you become seemingly lost, depressed and weary; like a man trying to eat all his meals with both hands tied behind his back. Depression means you are not consciously accessing the myriad impressions which your soul is giving you every moment, and which make you excited about living.

Your ego would like you to believe that you are on some profoundly complex search. Actually, the solution is to get the Energy flowing through your body so that you can connect to these impressions once again. Whatever tools you use to help you to do this are fine, but it is essential-especially with the way the Energy is accelerating now-that you do so.

#106 **Affirmation**

Today is the day in which I align all aspects of my life - my physical health, my emotions, my resources, my relationships, my creativity - with what I truly desire. What I truly desire is what brings me the deepest joy; it is no more complicated than that.

To facilitate this alignment, I will not use my mind as the driving force. My mind will assume its proper role as a servant to the Divine Energy which is what I am, and which I now allow to create my life. When my mind comes up with its many tricks of distraction – when it teams up with its old friend fear to create a thousand doom and gloom scenarios - I will gently and lovingly remind it that I am the master. If my faithful body manifests that which I do not desire (from years of recording the drumbeat of my limitations), I will gently and lovingly remind it that those days are over, and that I am now moving in an entirely different direction. I will not expect my body to heal decades of conditioning in a day (although this can certainly happen). I will gently and lovingly give it the space to heal itself, as its cells are programmed to do.

If I doubt that any of this is possible, I will remind myself of how deeply it has always resonated within my soul. I will listen to the words of wise friends from Spirit, and of those messengers who have returned from beyond the veil. In their unique ways, each speaks of these same principles.

I will reach out as well as go within. I will not despair. I will receive love with equal measure as I give it.

I am magnificent.

I am holy.

I am Divine.

#107 A Simple Tool For Creating Miracles

This little technique is designed to be used anytime you have a thought, emotion or life condition which is upsetting to you. I have followed these five steps many times, and have created many miracles by doing so. The process was originally taught to me by The Ones With No Names, channeled by Flo Aeveia Magdalena. (I have modified it slightly).

1. Relax and allow yourself to truly feel whatever it is that is bothering you. This may not be as easy as it sounds. We have a tendency to fight what makes us uncomfortable (which only serves to magnify it). When we are not fighting we may be denying or running away; or feeding the "problem" by worrying and putting

energy into it. All of these reactions cause the concern to grow. Instead of fighting, resisting, running, or feeding; just try to be with whatever you are feeling. Accept the experience as it is and observe it as best you can. This posture is greatly enhanced by the act of breathing deeply "into" the feeling. Your breath provides the wings that take you into your own essence.

2. Thank the disturbing thought, emotion, sensation or life condition for bringing you its message! At first, this might be difficult. If you are in pain and you can't manage to "thank" your pain, just do the best you can.

Gratitude for what we are upset about is based on the assumption that everything we experience is trying to teach us what our soul seeks to learn. If we see our condition as a messenger that is trying to tell us something about how we can live our full potential; we move into a much more powerful position, then if we see ourselves as the victim. (As always, there is absolutely nothing that you can do "wrong" with any of these steps).

3. In step three, get the message! Feel what the challenging thought, emotion, sensation or condition is trying to teach you. This is the most important, and most deeply personal part of the process. You are the only person who can do this. It is not a mental process; nor does the sky have to open and serenade you with Celestial Music. Just relax, breathe, and try to FEEL what the particular issue is trying to teach you. At this point when I do the steps, I usually ask, "Please help me to understand what the message is here. What is this really all about"? "What am I teaching myself"? You can pray, send out a desire, or just feel out the answer; whatever is most comfortable. If no message comes, that is fine. You can try again another day. As I said, the message can be very subtle: You may get a feeling come over you like, "I know I have to start expressing myself more" or "I am trying to make everybody happy but myself", or "Whenever I am afraid to move forward in life, this physical symptom kicks up!"

4. After you have allowed yourself to accept and to feel what is bothering you (without fighting or feeding it), have thanked the

"problem" for bringing you its message, and have gotten the message; you are now ready to visualize the way you truly desire to be! Please don't get hung up on the word "visualize." If you are one of those people who tend to see images, that's fine; by all means, see yourself running through the field, breathing clearly, speaking confidently, loving yourself, staying calm and poised while others are arguing, etc. If you don't tend to see images, you can talk yourself through the process. I find that it is perfectly effective to say, "I am breathing deeply and joyfully," "I am initiating creative new projects," "I am behaving calmly despite what is going on around me," etc. Make it fun! Play with it !

5. The last step is one that I was told I really needed to do because I have a tendency to forget it. In this final step you take some kind of action in the physical world to ground the process here. This doesn't have to be a big deal. You could take a walk with your new found perspective. You could write something, draw something, say a prayer; take any action which reinforces in the material world the kind of person you are visualizing yourself as.

One more point. I have had great success using the fruits of this process as a practice in my everyday life; especially with physical symptoms. After I got the message, every time the physical symptoms would pop up, I would say to myself, "Thank you very much for giving me this message. I understand that you are trying to tell me that I am afraid to express myself in the world. I don't need you to give me this message anymore. We are doing things differently now)!" . This has been quite successful for me.

Well, that's it. Like I said, I have turned around some really difficult issues with this process. The key is to accept everything you are experiencing with lots of self-love and without judgment. As it says in A Course In Miracles, a miracle is simply "a shift in perception".

I wish you all many miracles in your lives!

#108 Any Thought

When a thought comes into your head, ask yourself two questions: Is this what I truly want from the deepest part of my being? Does this thought express my soul's deepest desire?

Do your best to stay out of self-judgment. Then, if the answer to these questions is "no," just let the thought go. Snap your fingers and let it go. Don't fight it, deny it or magnify it.

What greater authority could any thought have over you than your own calling to be who you truly are? The fear-based thoughts from your negative ego like to pretend they are authentic, but they are not. There is no use in fighting these imposters; just see them for what they are and answer the two questions above. In time even the most terrifying of them will lose their grip on you.

Then you become the master of your own consciousness.

#109 Encountering Suffering

A while ago I was struggling with a simple question. How do you connect with your own Divinity in the face of human suffering? When a good part of this world (or someone you care for deeply) is in pain; is it possible to feel the peace inherent in your own Divine nature? Are we abandoning our spouses, children, parents, or the millions who suffer horribly on this planet, if we experience peace in the face of their struggles? Even if we have the right to, how in the world can we?

These questions cannot be answered blithely, no matter what our cherished beliefs. Of course, the mind, fueled by deep emotion, has ready made answers. It will tell us that it is "wrong", even uncaring, to dare to feel our connection to the Divine in the face of the suffering of those closest to us. Or it will paralyze us with fear, so we are rendered incapable of feeling anything, and justify this paralysis in the name of a sacred duty.

In truth I believe the answer to these questions captures the deepest meaning of faith; not faith in a belief system, but faith in the stillness within us where our Divinity makes its presence known. In this space, all questions dissolve. In this space there is only love, in this space we find the strength to live, and to allow others the dignity to learn whatever they choose. We need not worry about what we feel when we connect to this space, for we will be living in touch with our deepest nature. We can be assured that we will not be abandoning or harming anyone, and that we are doing what is highest and best for all. In this space, we can rest in the great flowing river of life and in the everlasting knowledge that we are love.

In truth, if we desire to serve those who suffer, the best thing that we can do is to go to this place within ourselves as often as we can. This is not about denying or suppressing emotions. All emotions must be acknowledged and accepted. But when you continue to block your attunement through fear and attachment, it becomes far more difficult to help, no matter how much you might care. Believe me, when you are in pain, you prefer someone around you who is centered in their own sacredness. And yes, in the alchemy which inspires this beautiful universe, your centeredness may help them (and yourself) to heal.

#110 **My Spiritual Practice**

Someone once asked me, "what is your spiritual practice?" I replied, "doing the laundry".

I could easily have said, "making lunch, petting the dog, driving my car, taking a nap, buying groceries, reading posts on Facebook," etc. All would have been equally valid.

Every moment of the day there are thoughts and emotions that enter my consciousness to work (and to play) with. Some I allow

74

to pass through me, others inspire me to action. There is also an energy which underlies these thoughts and emotions. In every moment, I have the choice of whether I am going to relax into this energy and allow it to deepen, or whether I am going to cloud over it by obsessing about things on a mental level.

Here comes my old friend anxiety. Do I magnify it by fighting or cultivating it; or do I lovingly allow myself to feel it and let it go? Here comes some old emotional pattern, whispering that I need to do something in order to be approved of. What do I do with this deep, partially buried emotion? Do I allow myself to spin out and start feeling guilty about how "unspiritual" I am for feeling this way? Do I let it cloud my judgment and start to act from it? Or do I just acknowledge it, see it for what it is, love myself, and let it go?

The man down the street is having a bad day and yells at me while I am walking the dog, saying that the dog touched his grass? Do I nurture the reaction that is welling up inside of me? Do I act on it and yell back at him? Do I get down on myself for having this reaction and paralyze myself with guilt? Or do I simply do my best to breathe deeply, observe it, and acknowledge that I am something deeper than all this?

For me, this is what spiritual practice is all about. Don't get me wrong, meditation can definitely help us to replenish ourselves from the wellspring of energy which is our birthright. Yoga certainly helps us to align all of the levels. There are a myriad other disciplines that are enormously helpful. But the heart of my practice still gets back to doing the laundry; and to the consciousness that I cultivate as I put my clothes in the dryer, and as I make my way through the folding.

Ah, the folding.

Always the hardest part.

#111 **Yearning For Brussels Sprouts**

The best way I have found to change my weight is to change my consciousness. When I am filled with the excitement of living, I no longer need to fill myself with foods that do not nurture me. Much to my amazement, when I align with my soul's intent, I find myself yearning for Brussels sprouts.

#112 **Happiness**

I know what happiness is. For me there is no mystery about it. Happiness is the undistorted experience of my own being; of that foundational energy I feel when I am not deluding myself with fear. It's quite simple actually. It has nothing to do with buying a BMW, building a big house, winning the lottery, finding the woman of my dreams, or getting a book published. All these things might make me high; but the high is always short-lived. When I feel the abiding connection to the energy of what I am; I feel like Noah of old who we are told, "walked with God."

Walking with God, dancing with God, singing with God, playing with God, working with God, laughing with God (not as a Being apart, but as the life force within); all of this flows when we experience the essence of our own being (and we don't even need a concept of "God" to do so). When I am feeling this Divine energy, you may find me grinning ear to ear while cleaning the toilet. When my sense of connection is obscured (by the ego traps that I set for myself), I could be on a tropical island, with all my needs being met, and still make myself miserable.

I am still learning how to consciously walk with Source every minute. Yes, I know that I always do so because we are One, but knowing something intellectually is not the same as consistently experiencing it.

I get caught up in the clouds sometimes. They waft over me without my even realizing it. Physical discomfort, emotional discomfort, sadness, fear, anger; all may obscure my experience of All That Is (if I allow them to). I understand, however, that I wouldn't know what the sun was, if it weren't obscured from time to time by the clouds. As my channeled friends like to say, "the darkness suggests the light". That's just how it is here. No sense compounding the problem by flagellating ourselves when we get caught up in the former.

All of this, I believe, serves a purpose. We come here and obscure what we truly are, so that we can find what we truly are, and somehow this makes it real for us. We come here to lovingly release the myriad obfuscations that we have invented and been taught since childhood. As more and more people learn to do this, I believe we reach a state of "critical mass". I am no authority on critical mass, but I sense that it means that the global energy around the earth which we operate in will buoy and sustain us, instead of dragging us down. I strongly sense, but cannot prove, that this is gradually happening. Heaven on earth is not a place but a consciousness.

And each one of us possesses the keys to the kingdom.

#113 Healing

People sometimes ask me if a sick loved one can be healed. I don't have the wisdom to know if a soul chooses to stay in the body, or if, having had quite enough of this world, it chooses to return to the great ocean of joy which awaits it upon "death."

It seems to me, however, that it is often the one who asks the question who needs healing - healing from the perceived terror of aloneness, healing from the ravaging fear that no one will ever care again, healing from the consuming fire that tells them that they cannot survive "on their own" - healing from the bottomless chasm of a seemingly unknowable future.

I do not know which ravages of the body will be healed, but I do know that there is a Divine Energy which, when aligned with, can heal the ravages of both mind and body. Indeed, this energy is what we are.

#114 Another Little Revelation About How To Deal With Fear

Today while driving through Southern Vermont (OK, I got lost again), I had a "mini - revelation" which I would like to share. We all know that when we try to do battle with unwanted thoughts, we only end up magnifying them because, as the cliche goes, "what we resist persists". We also know that it is best to relax, breathe deeply, observe, and allow these thoughts to pass through us.

What occurred to me today is that there is something else that we can do. In addition to acknowledging, observing and not resisting; we can consciously choose to wrap our true magnificence around our unwanted thoughts. By this I mean we can ask that we experience the thought or emotion from the perspective of who we really are, from the fullness of our being; and then allow this to unfold.

I tried this today when an old, deep fear kept cropping up. I said, "fine, I fully accept you; but I ask to experience you from the fullness of what I am". Then I turned this into a little affirmation: "I choose to experience this emotion in the full balance of my being".

A sense of joy began to fill me as i drove by the beautiful ponds and lush green fields. There was a "motion" to this practice.. I was no longer pushing anything away from myself. I was drawing my greater Divine self to me, and asking to experience the thoughts that frightened me from that perspective.

I believe I shall be doing a lot more of this!

#115   Moving Beyond Guilt

What is guilt but self hatred dressed in the garments of morality? Unlike remorse, an authentic form of introspection, guilt overwhelms the original moral intent, and uses it as a hammer to beat us into submission. This is precisely the reason guilt is so hard to deal with; it uses our inherent moral sense as justification, then distorts this sense and pummels us with it. Instead of leading to constructive action, guilt only serves to torture and paralyze.

When destructive thoughts arise, instead of compounding the illusion with guilt, why not seek the message? Why not gently ask yourself, "what has caused me to forget my inherent joy, my palpable connection with All That Is?"

The forgetting happens to us all. Instead of feeling guilty, why not ask to feel inspired? Then take some action toward this end. It can be as simple as a heart to heart conversation with a friend, or a little "self-talk" to remind you of who you really are. If you can move beyond guilt, then you can consciously reconnect with your own Divine essence. That essence is always waiting for you with open arms.

#116 Awareness

Can you feel your awareness, the dwelling place of your being? It is revealed to you in the spaces between your thoughts. It is not something you can grasp with your mind, nor is it intended to be a great mystery that you must solve. It is real, it is palpable; it is the energy you feel when you close your eyes and allow all your thoughts, feelings and sensations to pass through you. It is also who you truly are. People can help you to access who you truly are but there are no magic formulas, no required time frames, no secret passwords, that you need to know in order to enter the temple of your own being.

Once you consciously find this space, you discover that it has the power to dissolve all of your dramas. It does this in the simplest way possible; by allowing you to shift your perspective. All this means is that you experience your dramas **from awareness and as awareness,** rather than from your mind, which is intricately caught up in, and is the ultimate creator of your pain.

The truly remarkable thing is you don't have to do anything at all except observe your dramas from the perspective of awareness, and watch them dissolve on their own. Your awareness is the most powerful force in the universe. The dissolution will happen as quickly as you allow it to, based on your courage and your willingness to face whatever has trapped you, and to face it as what your really are. At first, being human, you will still likely feel the guilt or the fear that has been at the center of your dramas for a very long time. But the mere act of experiencing these dramas as awareness will in time (and this can happen very quickly) allow them to melt away.

It is as if the dramas breathe a sign of relief and say, "Thank God, she has finally gotten it. Now we can return to the nothingness from which we were born".

#117 **Death**

Growing up, my extended family owned a small private cemetery. It's care and upkeep meant a great deal to my aunts and uncles, and it was the focal point of many of their meetings. They would have countless discussions (and sometimes arguments) over where people were going to be buried, how much to spend on maintenance, and (the real biggie) what to do when people married out of the faith.

As a child, it seemed to me that my relatives were more concerned about where to put the bodies of their loved ones, than about coming together for celebrations! This bugged me no end. Now that I am as old as they were, I have learned to respect the path that each soul has chosen (and to stay focused on my own).

A few years ago I was asked if I would give up the burial plot that my parents had originally reserved for me next to them (and which I had not kept the payments up on). I happily agreed. You see, although my parents died years ago, I can feel them dancing in my heart as I write these words. In fact I can swear that Ma is standing right next to me. I have absolutely no doubt that their essences are very much alive. (And I really think they are far too busy to pay much attention to the condition of their former bodies). Although I wont judge anyone else, I have no interest in where my bones are placed. When I die, scatter me to the four winds. Let the little birds peck at me. Then I intend to have a rollicking party with the souls of my friends and loved ones, and let the stars sparkle to our laughter.

#118 **When Someone You Love Suffers**

To experience the pain of someone you love without fear means to let go of your own needs and be in complete presence with that person. This is never easy, and we need to lovingly allow ourselves the time and space to do this as best we can. To be fully present is the most precious gift which we can offer to another. Our fear is not for the person who suffers but for ourselves. It is borne of the fear-based ego, which screams that we cannot live unless the one we love exists in the form which it demands. What is really feared is our own aloneness. And this fear must be accepted without judgment.

There is a deep peace in this fearless love, tinged with sorrow. It is a peace born of the understanding that this finite drama is but a disguise, and that true perfection exists, even in the midst of profound human pain. In this peace we afford each person the dignity to learn as they choose, and we offer heart and hand with compassion and honor.

#119 A Different Path To Knowledge

How do we acquire knowledge? Let us say we are given a piece of information from a source that we have great respect for. For purposes of this discussion let us say that we are told, "There is no time. Everything you perceive is happening at the same moment. The human nervous system superimposes the concept of linear time on these perceptions because that is the way it operates in this dimension".

Now suppose you are trying to gain a deeper awareness of this whole business of timelessness. You really want to "get it". What do you do? Well most likely you will set to thinking about it. You will try to analyze the notion with your mind, based on your past experience. You may even have an "aha moment" where you actually feel the validity of the concept, rather than simply speculate about it.

In my experience there is another entirely different approach to gaining knowledge. This approach receives almost no respect because most people have little experience with it. Nevertheless, I have found that it is the most dependable and fulfilling of all. Quite simply, what I am referring to is acquiring knowledge by experiencing the underlying energy of your being, and gradually becoming consciously aligned with this energy. As the ego-based thoughts and emotions which comprise your sense of "self" slowly yield to the vibrating river of energy at your core; ideas that you once strained to figure out intellectually suddenly begin to make sense. Their truth is experienced on a much deeper level than what you are used to. You haven't "figured anything out" by an intellectual process. You have simply freed yourself from some of the illusions which had captivated you, and you are beginning to experience clarity from aligning with the foundational energy of your essence.

This is a difficult process to explain because we are so conditioned to think that, in order to know something, we must analyze it with our minds. I am not criticizing this approach. I am simply saying that there is another approach which can sometimes be much more rewarding. If I want to "get" such concepts as "we are One", "there is no judgment", "everything is happening at once", "I am a part of God"; I do not spend a whole lot of time thinking about them. Nor do I read too many books on metaphysics. I know that the validity of these concepts will gradually become known to me on a much deeper level as I learn to open to and to integrate the energy which is at the root of my being.

So, for me personally, if I really want to understand the concept that "there is no time"; I simply allow myself to grow into that understanding on an energetic level. The best way that I can truly comprehend this concept is to continue to accept and observe my ego-based thoughts and emotions, deepen my conscious connection to the underlying energy of my being, and live my life. This path produces its own "aha moments". Knowledge creeps into the very cells of your being and you find yourself saying, "that's obvious" about the things that once totally puzzled you.

#120 The Essential Alrightness Of The Universe

You cannot feel rejected when you are aligned with your own being. The essential alrightness of the universe fills your consciousness regardless of what anyone says or does. Anger, hurt feelings, envy, fear, self-pity are incompatible with the ever deepening sense of peace you feel when you become one with the flowing current of what you are.

It doesn't matter. You embrace what others say or do, and your own painful reactions, with a great big abdominal smile. You are palpably held and buoyed by the ecstatic universe that you are one with. You don't have to earn the right to feel this way, twist yourself in knots, or climb the highest mountain. All that is required is that you be honest with yourself, lovingly accept what you feel, and (as my channeled friends like to say) affirm that you are light and light you shall remain.

We have become so removed from our own Divine essence, that we have projected this essence as existing outside of ourselves. In truth there is no "outside" or "inside". There is only the vibrating Light of Creation which we are a part of.

I believe this is a cause for celebration.

#121 **The Choice**

The choice is ours whether we wish to focus on the unraveling of the old order or the rebirth of the new. The challenge we face is that the de-structuring of existing conditions is accelerating, and we are being bombarded with images associated with this de-structuring on a daily basis. The mind seizes upon these images and (because it works in codependence with our conditioned fears) causes us to feel a surge of helplessness. Our fear-based ego would love for us to believe that the great unraveling is all that is.

But it is not. In reality the unraveling is a symptom-a terrifying symptom for those who are caught up in it- but a symptom of a much greater process. This process is nothing less than the flowering of the consciousness that we call "Heaven on Earth."

The challenge is compounded by the fact that the only evidence we may experience of this great unfolding is a profound feeling within the silence beneath our thoughts. We humans (particularly we males) have been taught to totally disregard such intuitions. We have been conditioned to believe that they have nothing to do with the "real world". We were never taught how to trust or to create from the energy which is at the core of what we, and all things, are. Indeed, if at one time in our lives we experienced the beauty and the majesty of this force, we were quickly told to "get back to reality".

All of our fears may come pouring into us when we see the images of horror on our television sets and computer screens; fertile ground for the fear-based ego to weave its spell. "All is lost", "What good is your vaunted inner growth now?", "Why do you continue to hide your head in the sand like a fool?"

In the face of all this is a deep knowing; a knowing which at times seems to defy the very logic of survival. Yet this knowing not only coexists with our fears; it grows palpably stronger with each moment.

I suggest that trusting this knowing is not only a supreme act of faith, but an act of the deepest realism. This does not mean that we escape from the world. It means that we truly engage in the world, grounded in the abiding sense that we are part of the great unfolding tapestry of Creation.

#122 **Self Love**

"Just as the key to my healing was unconditional self-love that eliminated fear, the key to a better world is for everyone to care for themselves the same way, realizing their true worth." ——Anita Moorjani, Dying To Be Me

Today I was feeling stressed and this got me to thinking about the importance of self love and its expression through self-care. It suddenly dawned on me that loving and caring for myself was not simply a means to help me to stay healthy, although that was certainly a big part of it. No, for me, the most important reason was even more fundamental. In fact, you could say it was and is the most important thing in the world to me.

When I care for myself I am able to BE myself, and what could possibly be more important than that? I am able to consciously align with the deepest, truest, most authentic aspect of my being that I can experience at this time. When I lose my sense of connection to self (by not taking care of myself), I also lose the palpable feeling of love and wellbeing which inspires me to serve others.

If I take on more than I can handle, or get caught up in too much stress, I am like a person who walks into a room with a beautiful set of clean clothes, and comes back a muddy mess. There is an art to listening to what the soul truly needs, to assist it in blooming on this earth. This voice is often drowned out by a host of "shoulds" and moral judgments that we have been taught, and have internalized, since childhood. When all the shoulds try to seduce us, it is wise to remember that, as Anita Moorjani suggests, the very best thing that we can do for others is to be who we really are. And the way to stay in touch with who we really are, is to love and care for ourselves enough to make our connection to our own loving essence the most important thing in our lives.

#123 Creating Our Own Reality

I see people "creating their own reality" all the time. I see people, friends of mine, clinging to the unshakeable belief that this is a dog eat dog world; that everyone is out to get something from them. Does it come as any surprise that these people are constantly co-creating situations in their lives that serve to justify these beliefs?

I am not talking about people who are born into such horrific conditions that, in practical human terms, the notion of "creating your own reality" rings hollow. I do believe in that principle, and I believe that all souls create exactly what they need. It would, however, be grossly insensitive for me to blithely talk about spiritual principles under those circumstances.

I am talking about people whose basic material needs are being met and who, it seems to me, hold themselves back by blaming their parents, the government, rich people, poor people, or even the human race in general. They blame everyone and everything possible outside of themselves, and they don't realize how these beliefs continue to imprison them, and keep them from realizing their own power as aspects of All That Is.

I am not naive. I would be the first to admit that our socio-economic systems (all of them) are profoundly out of balance. Powerful people, lost in their egos, willingly separate themselves from and abuse others. These systems are entrenched, but they are cracking under the strain.

There is, however, an energy available to us which will allow us to thrive and - to use a metaphor from the Old Testament - to "walk with God". By raising our vibration, by acknowledging the patterns which no longer serve and letting this energy flow through our bodies, we not only thrive as individuals, but collectively we create new systems that respect and nurture all.

#124 The Coinage Of Belief

One of the leading websites dealing with spirituality is called Beliefnet.com. I find the name to be instructive because it assumes that beliefs lie at the core of the spiritual experience. This assumption seems to inform everyday life as well. If someone wants to know what "spiritual path" you are on they will commonly ask "what do you believe?"

I have been advised by my channeled teachers to hold as few beliefs as possible. Their advice rings true.

As far back as I can remember, I came to the conclusion that the coinage of belief was cheap. It always seemed to me that what many people believed (and in some cases would die for) was largely the product of what they had been taught or conditioned to accept; not what they had actually experienced. Back in junior high school, it occurred to me that the people who professed great certainly in a particular religious belief, would probably be just as committed to a seemingly contradictory belief, had different parents picked them up from the hospital at birth. The devout Muslim might be telling folks that they had to accept Jesus into their hearts to escape eternal damnation. The Orthodox Jew might firmly believe that Mohammed was the Messenger of Allah. The Hindu might now be proclaiming that Catholicism was the one true religion.

There is a vast difference between beliefs and direct experience. Consider the first hand accounts of near death experiencers. NDE'rs do not tell us that they believe that life continues after death, or that they believe that they encountered a Light of indescribable love. They tell us that they know these things with the deepest and most powerful knowing. Research has shown that these experiences have a profound impact on them; much more profound than any of the beliefs that they previously professed. This is because these experiences do not come from a mental/emotional level; but from a much deeper level; what many of us refer to as the soul.

I believe (there I go again) that we are moving from a belief-based spirituality to an experience-based spirituality, and I am quite happy about this. After all, I have never met an NDE'r who came back and said, "Thank God I'm Presbyterian and not Methodist"!

#125 "I Will Pray For You"

"I will pray for you".

How many times have you heard this before?

Sometimes it is said in a perfunctory manner, not because of any terrible insincerity on the part of the speaker, but simply because it is the only way out of an awkward situation. Other times, the speaker may express a genuine desire, and may actually go home and say a prayer. (I must confess, I wonder how high the correlation actually is between those who make the statement and those who do the deed).

By all means please do pray for me. I graciously accept your prayer. I do, however, have one request. Please do not incorporate into your prayer an image of me which is less than the magnificent being that I truly am. You see, when you do this - when you project a vision of me that is less than whole - you help in some small way to make this vision real. I am not saying that I am a helpless victim of your thoughts; but your limited vision makes it a teeny bit more difficult for me to express the power and beauty of my being. If you doubt my thesis, consider how you feel when someone looks at you with pity, versus how you feel when someone looks at you with genuine respect.

Here's my preference. I would greatly prefer that you not visualize me in a desperate state, and then ask God to lift me out of my misery. (I have created enough desperate states over the years without anybody having to add to them energetically). Instead, I would ask that you use your ability as a creator to visualize me as the joyful, healthy, dynamic being that I truly am. If I am limping, see me running. If I am in pain, visualize me dancing joyfully across the ballroom floor. If I am confused, picture me clear eyed and at perfect ease.

Our thoughts do effect each other. (Especially since the "other" is actually the same as "us"). Every time you think a limited thought about someone, you send that energy out to them. Some people know better than others how to let that energy pass through them.

Your ego may resist when you choose to move beyond the familiarity of pity. There is a certain sense of security in the separation you experience when you feel sorry for someone (because thank God, it isn't you)! To see the person in their true glory, you have to encounter them for who they are, and this can be scary. It means you have to actually believe in the Divinity which you pray to and which is in all things. You have to affirm, despite what everything may look like, that all is well; that you are encountering a spark of Light, which deserves the deepest respect and admiration, regardless of how they are choosing to learn at the moment.

#126 **Authenticity**

For me, being authentic does not mean "doing what I feel". I am a frail human and I feel and think all kinds of crazy stuff. My emotions can be dramatically effected by things as innocuous as the temperature outside, having to get up early, or the dog not answering when I call. Indeed, contrary to the old sixties mantra; not always doing what I feel is an essential aspect of my spiritual growth. It is one of the keys that has allowed me to open to the expression of my soul's purpose here on the earth plane.

Don't get me wrong. Not always doing what you feel should not be confused with repressing what you feel. Repressing, running from or fighting uncomfortable thoughts only makes them more powerful; so does feeding them, nurturing them and acting them out. What I choose to do, what allows my energy to truly move, is to only nurture and act on those thoughts which express the deepest, most authentic part of my being that I am aware of.

For example, yesterday the real temperature where I live rose to over ninety degrees. I had tasks that I wanted to accomplish and I stuck with them, but by late afternoon I was feeling overwhelmed and frustrated. Obsessive thoughts and uncomfortable emotions started to come into my consciousness. I have learned not to beat myself up about such moods, but to simply allow them to be and observe them. To me, authenticity does not mean putting energy into any condition that I find myself in or acting out of it. It means accepting the state, but also exercising discernment. So I asked myself, "what exactly is going on here? Why do I feel the way I do?" The answer was quite obvious. I was under physical and emotional stress, and I was not consciously in touch with the deepest aspect of my being. So I made a little statement to myself, "surface thoughts and disturbing emotions floating through. These do not express the deepest, clearest parts of my consciousness." Then I lovingly let the thoughts and emotions flow through me.

Authenticity to me means remembering who I am and trying to stay true to that. It does not mean believing in or being held captive by any thought that happens to come into my head.

#127 **The Design**

One of the great joys of my life at this time is that I can finally feel the unfolding of my soul's design in the world. I don't use these words metaphorically or to express a "belief".
It is a profound experience which is inherent in that energy that I often speak of; the foundational energy which moves "underneath" the play of my thoughts and emotions. There is a sense of what Lama Sing (a group of beings channeled by Al Miner) refer to as "joyous expectancy". There is the resurrection of long abandoned dreams, the rebirth of hope, the flowering of purpose.

The mind rebels. It senses the deep movement of the river of life and resists. Or it is attracted to what it wants and seeks to make things happen. But the great river has its own order. It's energy serves what is highest and best. If I step back and allow the current to flow, I can feel the river carrying everything I need to me, to fully express my soul in the world. I do not need to be certain of the forms in which my soul's dreams are being realized (resources, relationships, time frames are glimpsed but not fully known), but that just adds to the delight. All that is needed is to know, with the deep knowing that comes from the energy which inhabits the spaces between my thoughts. This knowing fills my heart with unending gratitude.

#128 **Judgment**

91

What is judgment? It is an act of separation; an obscuring of the inherent connection between two human hearts. When we judge we allow a curtain to fall between us and the "other". We turn our backs, avert our eyes, and shut down the flow of Divine Energy which is what we truly are. Judgments are not harmless. They carry a charge, and when they are multiplied millions of times over, they contribute to the density which still holds much of the planet in its grip. This is why Jesus and the great Masters spoke out so strongly against judging.

We are part of a force of profound compassion. Divinity does not judge or separate from us, or from those we perceive to be the vilest of criminals. Can we not oppose someone's destructive action, without building a wall around our hearts? Who needs our clear-eyed love more than the one who is so lost to his own essence, that he would commit a horrible crime?

If, as near death experiencers tell us, The Light itself never judges, then by what authority dare we?

#129 Spiritual Maturity

Your spiritual maturity is not measured by your understanding or by how well you can articulate that understanding. It is measured by the choices you make when you are put to the fire; when your body is angry and your emotions yearn to escape, blame others, or wallow in dependency.

At these moments there is but one question.

Can you remember who you are?

#130 Abundance

For those of us who are interested in attracting more abundance into our lives (and I assume that would include most of us), I recently had a wonderful reading with The Ones With No Names (channeled by Flo Aeveia Madgalena) that touched upon this question.

TOWNN shared a very interesting point that I had never given much thought to. Essentially they said that the idea that we only attract resources into our lives as an exchange for a service or product, actually restricts the flow of resources which are potentially available from the universe. If we think that resources, including money, only come to us as a quid pro quo for selling a painting, a book, or a CD; we tend to limit what we can receive to that one form of exchange. (Such a belief is something that most of us were deeply conditioned into accepting). This actually tends to make it more difficult for the universe to weave its magic!

For example, let's say we give a piece of jewelry we made to our cousin for her birthday. She then wears it to a dinner party, at which time her boss falls totally in love with it, and subsequently shows it to a friend who happens to own a string of boutiques and decides to order 500 pieces! (Well this is my example, but you get my drift). TOWNN strongly suggested that I sever any hold that the concept that resources only come as a direct exchange still has on me; and that I say the following affirmation (or something like it): "All of my resources come from the endless abundance of the universe. I open myself to the mystery of how I am going to receive them)".

The vibration of being open to the flow, and willing to receive the mystery, liberates us from the limitations of form imposed by our belief system.

Wishing you all the abundance that you so richly deserve!

#131   Pushing Buttons

Often I hear someone say, "I didn't really mean to react the way I did, but that person really pushes my buttons".

What an interesting turn of phrase, this "push my buttons" is! It is worth taking a moment to look at the assumptions that lie behind it.

If someone can indeed "push your buttons" then you really are not responsible for your own reactions. When I push a button to turn on my computer, my computer does not have much choice as to how it is going to react. It cannot decide, "Hmmmm, I think Ted has been surfing the Internet too much lately, I'm going to just ignore him, no matter how much he pushes my button, until he gives up". The computer is totally powerless in the face of the mighty button pusher!

I try to remember that nobody can really push my buttons; all they can do is trigger me to do so myself. Now if somebody hits me over the head with a board and I scream, I admit that screaming was not really much of "a choice". But in the vast majority of cases I find myself in, I am truly my own button pusher!

#132   **A Diagnosis Of Cancer**

I was reading a while ago that Angelina Jolie was going to have another preventative cancer surgery. The article didn't specify the nature of the surgery, but I assume it is to prevent ovarian cancer which is also associated with the gene which she carries. I am certainly not judging her. I can clearly understand how she would assume, from a purely logical point of view, that her choice was best for herself and for her children.

Around twenty years ago I was diagnosed with testicular cancer. I was told in no uncertain terms that I needed to have one of my testicles removed. In those days (I don't know if the technique is different now), they could not do a biopsy, because the procedure had too high a risk of spreading the cancer. Two ultrasounds showed a definite lump in one of the testicles. The diagnosis was unequivocal. The ultrasounds confirmed what a physical exam had shown.

I was given no wiggle room. The Urologist told me I had a 99 per cent chance of having testicular cancer. I was also told that this type of cancer is fast growing and there was no other option but to have the testicle removed immediately. My primary doctor (who had referred me to the specialist) scheduled another appointment with me after I had gotten the Urologist's diagnosis. He asked me when I was scheduling the surgery and I replied that I had not decided whether I was going to have it. I will never forget his parting words: "Ted", the good doctor said, "you need to schedule this surgery. I'd hate to see you commit suicide."

Well, I never did the surgery and twenty years later I am fine. There is no question that if I did have testicular cancer it would have terminated my physical existence a long time ago. That's simply a medical fact. The little lump is still there; the same size as it was twenty years ago, and I never pay any attention to it.

My decision not to have the surgery was compounded by the fact that all the docs were telling me that surgery for testicular cancer had a very high success rate and that my chances for a full recovery were excellent. Of course my mind used this information to try to convince me that, not only was I nuts, but a complete idiot as well. Even some of my metaphysical friends were telling me to have the surgery. One woman I know (who actually had an NDE and wrote a book about it around 30 years ago) told me that if I didn't have the surgery, the next time she saw me I would probably be "in a box". (Not helpful).

So why didn't I have the surgery? The answer might surprise you. It wasn't because I believed that I could heal myself through alternative means (not that I am opposed to alternative medicine). The fact is, after I made my decision, I didn't do that much differently, except to forget about the issue and let go of the fear. (Of course, that was no small matter)!

I didn't have the surgery because of the incredible spiritual energy I felt coming into me. It was and is a palpable vibrating force. It seems to have a "destination" of its own, and when I don't block it, it opens up great vistas of peace and purpose. I chose not to have the surgery because - despite the weight of logic, reason and medical science impinging on me - I knew that getting cancer was incompatible with the flow of this energy and the direction it was taking me. I just knew it. I didn't "believe" it.

Let me make it very clear that I am not suggesting that anyone who is facing a similar diagnosis do what I did and forego surgery! Most likely, if you have a diagnosis like mine and you do not have surgery, you are going to die. (I have nothing against dying; while I embrace physical life, the bliss of Spirit is something I am very much looking forward to). But before you move into the bliss of Spirit, you will likely undergo deep physical and emotional suffering. That is not something I wish to see for anyone.

Because of the vibrating, pulsating energy within me, I was sure that I would be fine. I believe it is quite rare to experience this energy all day like I do. I don't believe I cured cancer; I just felt it was incompatible with the Force that was becoming the central focus of my life. It seemed to me that cancer simply could not co-exist with this Energy. Period.

The docs will say that I was one of the lucky one per cent. I only write this piece because I do believe that this kind of an experience needs to be shared; at the very least to offer a tiny bit of balance to all the other stuff that we are constantly bombarded with.

I am here.

I am alive. I am well.

Some would say, I am still crazy after all these years.

And I continue to thank that magnificent force that vibrates at the core of my being and leads me beside the still waters of life.

#133 **Commitment**

Your commitment to living from the River of Life takes precedence over the entire arsenal employed by the negative ego. The time may come when the River becomes so powerful that you will not be able to resist it anymore and maintain your sanity. This is the moment when you begin to awaken to the true joy of living.

Once again we refer to looking to the feeling tone of your thoughts, rather than to their logical content. The art of listening to what our thoughts feel like has never been seriously entertained in our culture. It has been sacrificed over and over again at the altar of the mind, and collectively we are paying the price for it.

Guilt is the greatest weapon which the negative ego employs to try to keep us from consciously flowing in the Great River of Life. There is no more seductive arrow in the negative ego's quiver than guilt. This is because guilt uses our own ethics, our own sense of "right and wrong" against us as a weapon. Guilt can rapidly turn into obsession and it can effect a stranglehold on the life force. It is an oppressive illusion, weighing you down, pushing your mind into overdrive.

The most important thing to remember (and they probably never taught you this in Sunday School) is that the very act of releasing the guilt soaked illusion (or any other negative emotion which traps you) sets in motion the resolution of whatever it was that you were feeling guilty about. By releasing the illusion that binds you and keeps you from flowing freely in the moment - you are consciously returning to the River of Life - the most powerful force in the universe. A guilt induced mind could never resolve an issue the way the Great River can. All you ever need to do is release the stranglehold which guilt has on you, and wait for a genuine impression from the River to guide you. The River knows when it is highest and best to call someone up that you think you offended, and when that act will simply make matters worse. The River knows if you need to correct that information you put down incorrectly on a form because you were afraid of losing something; or when it is highest and best to simply let it be. But to trust in the River you must allow your faith in its wisdom to supersede your mind's logic - even perhaps what it considers to be the "right" course to take - and to surrender to a higher Divine logic. This is the deeper meaning of faith.

#134 **Judgment Day**

Here is something I wrote in response to a man who was genuinely questioning the idea that there is no judgment after death, and who said it was hard for him to believe that "you can rape, or kill people and you wont have to pay for it".

Oh you do have to pay for it my friend. You pay for it everyday by being in a consciousness so removed from the experience of God/Goddess/All That Is, that you would be moved to do such things. You pay for it because you have lost your sense of joy and tenderness; you have obscured your connection to what you truly are and succumbed to the fear-based illusions of your mind. You "pay for it" when you leave your body and understand more clearly the ways in which you have denied your own nature. You pay for it when you relive the pain that you have co-created with others, and are faced with the undeniable truth that these are your brothers and sisters, made of the same Light as you.

Yet still there is no judgment. What good would it possibly serve to add condemnation or judgment, when these are the very forces which served to make you lose yourself in the first place? You are still loved beyond measure, because those who are trying to help you ARE love, and know nothing but love. They have absolutely no need to "punish" you. Their sole wish is to help you understand more deeply how to express the love that you are.

#135 A Funny Thing Happened To Me On The Way To My Soul

A funny thing happened to me on the way to my soul. I found that if I simply allowed myself to be with my fears and unwanted thoughts, to experience them deeply without reacting - and to affirm the deeper underlying reality of joy - my fears dissolved and I began to experience the magnificent flow of energy which is what I am. This was such a profoundly simple process, that my poor brain could not wrap itself around it. Yet it worked. Every time I had the courage to do it, it worked.

Let us say you have the thought, "I am worthless. I will never amount to anything". Before you even give yourself a chance to fully experience that thought, you start to react. Your body tenses, your emotions kick into overdrive, your mind starts to weave its endless embellishments. Or you begin to deny and resist; to pretend that you are not having the thought, to try to talk yourself out of it, to find something to escape into. In this dizzying dance of denial and magnification, you often forget the simplest, most challenging thing there is; to allow yourself to feel whatever it is that you are feeling (and to affirm that your deepest most magnificent self underlies it all).

The only way I know to do this is to breathe deeply into your thoughts and emotions. The breath is the beacon which lights your way through the illusion of darkness into the clarity of your own being.

#136 Faith

For decades I have been able to feel a vibrating, pulsating energy in the stillness between my thoughts. This energy does not feel like it is limited to my own consciousness. It feels like l am hooked into something far more global, although my own emotions can color it.

These days it feels like this energy is intensifying at a dizzying pace. If one can get a handle on integrating it with the emotional, mental and physical levels-and bringing it down through the body-the potential for joy and soul fulfillment is profound. On the other hand, the potential for "learning lessons" is also profound; because the energy will push out all of the deepest patterns that get in the way of its expression. There is nothing "wrong" with any of this. It can certainly be uncomfortable at times, but if we keep our focus on the message rather than the discomfort, we can move through it gracefully.

Now is the time to remember who we are, what we came here to do, and how much we are truly cherished by Creation; even when our minds, bodies and emotions may be screaming the opposite . This, it seems to me, is the true meaning of faith.

#137 **A Little Experiment**

Instead of fighting, denying or magnifying the thoughts and emotions which you don't like, try something different. Step back and say to yourself, "I choose to view these thoughts from the expansiveness of my being." You may use the terms "awareness" or "consciousness" instead of being, whatever you feel comfortable with.

What does it mean to make the simple choice to experience your thoughts and emotions from your awareness or being? It means that, to the best of your ability, you get in touch with the joy, safety, purposefulness, beauty, compassion and creativity of the Universal Energy of which you are a part. Then you simply shift perspective, because the reactive, terrifying, unwanted thoughts are now being observed by you, instead of controlling you or driving you crazy. You have made the decision to watch those terribly anxious thoughts as if you were in a play and you were performing the starring role!

The good news is this really works. And best of all, if you do this for a while (and it doesn't have to be for that long), the destructive or scary thoughts melt away on their own. Remember that A Course In Miracles says a miracle is "simply a shift in perception from fear to love." I would say that if you chose to make your stand from the fullness of your being than the love is automatic.

This is what I am doing at a very crucial, and super intense time in my life. If you care to try it, I would love to compare notes with you.

#138 **Worry Stories**

I inherited the gene for imagining the worse case scenario in every situation from my mother's side of the family.

My mother was a lovely woman, but a major league worrier. One day I decided to "teach" her something. I said, "Ma, how many things have you worried about in the past year". She thought for a moment and replied, "Maybe 500″. Then I said, "Of those 500 things you worried about, how many of them actually happened"? She thought again for a moment and replied, "None of them". Then just when I thought I had zeroed in on my grand teaching moment, she added (without missing a beat), "So far, thank God."

The good news is that I have grown to the point where I can recognize many of my worry stories and let them go, before they cut me down. I think I am doing pretty well with this.

So far thank God.

#139 **The World**

I am finding it necessary to stay aloof from much of the news transmitted via the media these days. Some would criticize me for "hiding my head in the sand". Perhaps, but it feels more like I am acting out of self-love and, indeed, self-preservation.

I still have things to do here. Being constantly bombarded by the vitriolic energy of separation, and the violent images that such energy creates, will not help me to align with what I am, nor will it help me to carry out my soul's purpose in this world. In fact, if I get caught up in this energy, it will do the exact opposite.

I believe that the destruction that we are witnessing (or de-structuring, if you will) is itself a response to the acceleration of Divine energy on this planet. It is the explosion which occurs when this energy is encountered by old patterns and beliefs. I've worked too hard and I've learned too much to allow myself to be seduced by it.

#140 **The Terrorist**

The most relentless terrorist I have ever encountered is my own mind. The negative ego employs an endless array of weapons in its desperate attempt to hold the territory that it claims. It's most seductive tactic is hijacking; stealing one's sacred sense of being, and supplanting it with lies. It spends many, many years laying down land mines of guilt, shame and fear. These it regularly explodes when it senses that we are coming closer to expressing our true being. It cannot be blamed for doing what it does, for without its service there would be no real growth in the human experience; no catalyst to push us to remember our Divinity.

It is best not to fight this little brother; not to run from it, magnify it, or act out of it. It is best to simply see it for what it is. Its only power comes from fear. When we choose to look at it fearlessly, when we simply breathe into it and acknowledge it for what it is, it disappears back into the shadows.

Then we can thank it for helping us to experience the truth of what we are. Indeed, what greater gift has anyone ever given us?

#141 Ego

What is ego?

Ego is a construct-a conglomeration of responses which, at a very early age, we come to consciously identify as "self". It is not the all expansive Self that we experience when we die; but it is created from this awareness. Indeed, since this awareness is All That Is, where else could ego come from?

Without this thing called ego, we couldn't even eat a carrot on this earth plane. In my opinion, even if you accept on a mental level that ego is not the ultimate reality, you still function through it while in the body; otherwise you could not function at all.

Indeed, the more we fight against the ego the more it clamors to be heard. The main reason the ego gets such a bad rap is that it is infused with emotions which we are learning to transform (fear, shame, guilt, self-hate, etc). The way to transform these emotions is to acknowledge and fully love them. This doesn't mean we have to act from them or indulge them; but once we lovingly accept them as part of our humanness, it is amazing how quickly they dissolve into the underlying, all encompassing magnificence of being.

#142 Discernment

One of the most important things I have learned on my spiritual journey is to pay attention to the feeling tone of my thoughts and not allow their logical content to determine whether I should put energy into them. The mind and the negative emotions (fear, shame, guilt, rage, etc) are codependent. The mind provides the "logical" structure or rationalization, while the emotions (often barely conscious) provide the fuel or juice. This can be a very potent combination because, unless we have learned to observe what our thoughts feel like, we can be easily seduced.

As someone who has had to deal with my share of obsessive thoughts, I have had to learn to pay particular attention to the feeling quality of a thought, not simply to its intellectual content. I can't say that I have mastered this, but I am getting pretty good at it. When fear has me in its clammy grip, I have learned to stop and ask myself a simple question. What do these thoughts feel like? Regardless of how justified my mind would like me to believe they are, I have learned that if they feel fearful and paralyzing (unless it is a rare moment of real physical danger); it is always best to let them go.

The mind would like you to believe that something terrible will happen if you allow the fearful thoughts to pass through you. Ironically, the exact opposite is true. When you allow the illusion of fear to dissipate, you get back into the flow of your being, which allows you to experience things with far greater clarity. You may (or may not) eventually address the issue that you were in such a tizzy about; but you will do so from a place of peace. The great irony is that from this new perspective, the solution to your problem is usually quite obvious; it was your fear which was preventing you from seeing it.

I said in an earlier entry (but it bears repeating) that sometimes I have to simply admit that fear has got to me, and that the best thing that I can do is to completely forget about an issue, until I get a clear impression from the river of life as to what I should (or should not) do about it. If I truly let an issue go, and trust that the answer will find me, it always does. I have seen this principle work, over and over, every time I have had the courage to apply it.

#143 **More Thoughts About Healing**

Breathing into the spaces of our discomfort, accepting and allowing, going ever deeper; this is what restores our true power. Acceptance is the heat that melts the seemingly solid fears.

Many of us are very good at ignoring our fears, gritting our teeth and soldiering on. We think that we can overcome anything by the use of will power. All the while our deeper power remains locked in ice.
We only succeed in exhausting ourselves, because the power of our will is the limited power of our minds. The power we need to access is the power of Source. It is located in our solar plexus, what is known as the seat of the soul. We gradually release this power by breathing into and accepting our fears, so that they begin to fall away because nothing is holding them in our bodies anymore. Then we are filled with the Creative Energy of Life itself, freed from the musty chambers in which it has been held prisoner, free to course through our bodies and be expressed in the world.

#144 **Love**

The Ones With No Names channeled by Flo Aeveia Magdalena told me a long time ago that humans tend to have some strange beliefs around the subject of beginning or ending "relationships". Many tend to believe that there is a certain quantity of love which can be doled out to another person. If the form of that relationship shifts and the two are no longer together physically, then that love ceases and - if a person comes together with someone else - then that love proceeds to go to the other individual; all in a very linear manner.

But this belief flies in the face of the far greater reality of what we are. If one is evolving and growing into a deeper alignment with one's Divine nature, then the capacity for love only grows stronger.

Expanding love is inclusive by nature. **The form in which it is expressed in the physical world may shift**, but a loving heart remains a loving heart. **Love has no desire or need to shut down to one person in order for it to be opened up to another.**

The life force is not static. Agreements are completed, learnings are shared, new learnings are begun. But none of this has to involve loving less or calibrating the heart.

Love does not cease. In fact it is at its greatest when freed from the beliefs which keep it in chains.

#145 Arguments

The older I get, the less I want to convince anybody of anything. Arguing, it seems to me, is like waging war against yourself, with phantoms of your own creation. My heart longs to share a deeper place, a space beyond "right" and "wrong," where love and terror can be expressed without fear of negation. To enter this land I must give up my quest for victory. I must lay aside all my armor and my weapons.

For me this is the true meaning of courage.

#146 Honoring Your Soul

If you worked in the medical profession would you deliberately inject yourself with a virus in order to empathize with your patients? Of course not.

Then why do you feel guilty experiencing peace, joy and simple abundance in the face of human suffering? Are you more effective at helping others when you deny your own nature?

I do not advocate turning a blind eye to suffering. I simply say that there is no moral imperative to deny your soul's birthright in order to live and to serve.

Honoring your own Divinity is the single most important thing you can do to effectively serve others.

#147 **My Primary Responsibility**

Let me be clear. My primary responsibility on this earth is to the state of my own consciousness. Everything else flows from this. If I lovingly cultivate the thoughts and emotions which I put energy into; I am able to palpably feel the Divine Energy which flows beneath these thoughts and emotions, and to hear the impressions which are sparked by this Energy. You may call this narcissism; I call it discernment.

I did not come here to fix anything. I came here to express the yearnings of my soul in human form. As I learn to do so, I have a greater impact on a greater number of people. It happens naturally, without the ego having to strive for it.

As heartbreaking as the onslaught of the daily news may be, I cannot allow myself to be seduced by the intense emotional and physical de-structuring that I see happening around me. It is not that I "don't want to get involved". I deeply want to get involved, but on a different level; a level which my soul cries out is true. If I stay focused on hearing the ever deepening call of my own being; I receive instructions, if you will, as to where I can use whatever knowledge or wisdom I may possess for the greatest good. This path may not always placate my mind, my cultural and emotional conditioning, or my fears; but it serves both self and others in the highest way possible.

#148 **The Ego's Webs**

The negative ego weaves its seductive webs in many ways. The most prominent is to have us believe that what we are feeling and thinking at any given moment is the most authentic expression of who we are. Whether we are experiencing rage, self-pity, despair, obsession, or hopelessness; the negative ego wants us to believe that these conditions represent the deepest and truest expressions of our being. The aspect of our consciousness that we call the negative ego would like us to forget that we have ever felt differently - that we have known joy, peace, compassion and purpose - and that while we felt such conditions, we inherently knew that we were in touch with the deeper reality of our being. It seeks, above all, to obscure the memory of this knowing.

It is unwise to attempt to fight the ego, to grit our teeth and resist it. As we know, such resistance only makes it stronger. But we can see it for what it is, without judgment, and make the deep inner decision as to whether the fear, shame, guilt, anxiety, or anger that it generates represents the deepest aspects of our being. In order to do this we must fully accept everything that we feel. This practice is not about denying the ego, but simply seeing it for what it is.

Another favorite tool that the ego employs is to blame somebody or some thing outside of ourselves for whatever it is that we are experiencing. If everything that we are experiencing can be seen as offering us a message ; there is no greater way to **not** get this message than to blame something outside of ourselves. Blaming takes the focus completely away from whatever it is that are trying to teach ourselves. We can spend a great deal of time (indeed our entire physical life) lost in this particular trap.
The final trick which the ego likes to employ that I will mention here, is to try to get us to avoid our discomfort by escaping into some form of physical pleasure. Food, drugs, sex, etc...anything that provides direct pleasure to the physical body, can be used as a way of avoiding the "message" that our resistance or our discomfort is trying to convey.

Eventually, all of the ego's paths lead to the realization that there must be a better way. And, in my opinion, that way is to truly feel whatever it is that we are feeling-to love ourselves even if the feelings are challenging-and to decide at the deepest level of our being who we are and what we desire. We have the power to do this! By practicing this whenever the challenges arise, we reach a point where the thoughts that once plagued us are experienced in a totally different way. They may still arise from time to time, but now we can see them for what they really are; fleeting thoughts that no longer carry an emotional charge that ensnares us. Through this practice we free ourselves from being terrorized by the illusions of our own minds.

#149 Breaking The Cycle Of Disease

To those who are steeped in material reality - who draw their perceptions of what is possible solely from their physical senses - the existence of a vital life force at the core of our being is difficult to accept. The idea that we may create our own dis-eases, by blocking this energy through fear, is even harder to believe. Even for those who experience this energy, acknowledging our capacity to heal ourselves can be an enormous challenge.

Part of the problem is that dis-ease triggers a cycle that can be very hard to break out of. Pain immediately induces a response on the emotional level. Fear, despair, self-reproach, self-pity, denial, rage, helplessness; all can be triggered by a hurting physical body. Then the trusty mental body kicks in - fueled by these emotions - and it begins to weave its "logical" tales of woe. These tales are often supported by a medical profession which focuses solely on chronicling the patterns that diseases take in the physical realm. Does it surprise anyone that our diseases show these patterns when the mass consciousness is still ensnared in the limitations of what we perceive as physical reality? All of us are swimming in the same soup.

So the key question is, how do we break the cycle? I can't speak for anyone else, but I know that it is most helpful if I can still manage to believe in joy, excitement and soul expression; even when (especially when) alleged "symptoms" rear their head. The emotional juices and accompanying mental stories are like grotesque creatures whose poisonous tentacles literally freeze the body (and the flow of Energy) in place. This energy needs to be freed.

Not only is it highly recommended that we believe in our capacity for joy when we are able to (even when we might not feel it), but the key is to dare to express our souls, to make this great act of faith, to behave in a way that chooses to break the hold that the tentacles of the mind have on us. This doesn't mean that we have to avoid any treatment (conventional or alternative) that we believe might help us.

Too often we make the mistake of assuming that we need to break the hold that fear has on us first, and then express our joy, wisdom and inherent desire to serve. You could spend a very long time trying to do this. Act in a way which is consistent with having the chains already broken, and you might be surprised at how good you start to feel.

#150 Stand, Breathe, Feel And Affirm

The great joy of spiritual growth is to realize that the limiting thoughts and emotions which masqueraded as your true self, and which for so long imprisoned you, are just fleeting phenomena. Your entire being breathes a momentous sigh of relief, as you witness the chains that bound you inexorably losing their charge. With this release, the sacred energy of your essence is allowed to flow deeply into the spaces where once you were held in terror by your own thoughts.

You may rail against your limiting thoughts and emotions, you may declare war on them, you may curse and blame another, you may pretend these conditions do not exist, you may beg for help from the forces of grace that attend you; but until you stand, breathe and feel, you will never be free.

It is indeed the simplest of all practices, but it can be one of the most challenging when the illusion is strong. And while you stand and breathe and feel, you affirm - you affirm that, even as you allow yourself to feel the terror, you are indeed something much greater than this - you are a spark of magnificence, a perfect aspect of the Light of Creation.

This simple practice-stand, breathe, feel and affirm-will help to set you free (even if at first your mind rebels against it). Rest assured you will feel the same tired thoughts and emotions returning to ensnare you, but each time they come they will lose a little more of their power. Soon you will find yourself looking at them and thinking, "how could I have tricked myself with such ethereal thoughts and emotions; how could they have seemed so real? How could I have allowed these clouds to block the glorious sunlight of my true nature?"

Then you will begin to feel the great river of life flowing through you, blessing you with the purity of your own essence, and your heart will come alive to the everlasting dance of Creation.

#151 A Little Tool For Dealing With Fear

Fear, the great imposter, uses the mind as its handmaiden. Fear provides the juice and the mind provides the justification. The deep deception is that letting go of fear means that what we are afraid of will manifest.

In reality, nothing is farther from the truth.

Suppose you are working in your garden, entranced by the beautiful Spring day, and you look down and find a deer tick on your sleeve. Thoughts of debilitating Lyme Disease rush into your consciousness and you immediately brush the tick away. Then a half hour later you find another deer tick on your other sleeve. This time you feel a sick sense of panic as you brush the tick away once more. You go back into the house and your fear-based ego moves into overdrive.

Your "logical" mind, fueled by fear, begins to obsess about "solutions" to your dilemma. "Should I spray the yard? Oh I can't put those toxic chemicals down. Is there anything natural I can use. Wait let me Google that. Oh that stuff isn't powerful enough. What if I get Lyme Disease? What if I already have it? What if my house is infected? Do I need to use an insecticide bomb, Must I vacate for a few days?" I could go on and on. The mind provides an endless variety of issues to obsess about when fear offers its poisonous wellspring of fuel.

So here's the trick. It is, in my opinion, absolutely crucial that we get this and, indeed, once we do, it is a cause for great rejoicing! Letting go of the fear does NOT mean that we are letting go of resolving the issue itself; it just means that we are letting go of the fear that has enveloped the issue, and which prevents us from seeing it clearly, and taking appropriate action if necessary. The great irony is that the fear which we are afraid to let go of (because our mind tells us that something disastrous will happen) is itself what is preventing us from seeing the "solution" which is trying to unfold in the moment. Another way to say this is that, when we let go of the fear (which has used our logical mind to justify itself); we return to the flow of life, the great river of energy which provides us with clarity and direction for our lives.

Sometimes what I do, when I have allowed fear to paralyze me and I can't seem to let go of it, is to say to myself something like, "I know fear has me in its grip. I know this fear is an illusion and it is distorting the flow of life so I can't see clearly. Therefore I choose to let this fear go for one day (or more if necessary). I do this to regain my perspective-to get back into the flow. In one or two days time i will reflect on the issue, with peace and clarity, and then take appropriate action if necessary".

I know that even the step outlined above is not really necessary if you truly are living your life fearlessly. I know that all I really need to do is let go of the fear and surrender to the flow of life and the answers will always present themselves. But sometimes I use the little tool above (and I write it all down to make it more real for me). It can be very helpful. The important thing is to remember that you are NOT letting go of addressing the issue that needs addressing; you are letting go of the fear that is actually keeping you from addressing the issue that needs addressing! In my opinion, it is very, very helpful to be able to see through this deception which the fear-based part of your ego is trying to seduce you with.

#152 Thoughts On Prayer

If you are praying to be free of a condition, no matter how much those who are attendant upon you may wish to help, they are limited by the fact that you are the Master of your own consciousness (whether you are aware of this or not). You are responsible for the conditions in your life, so-as challenging as these conditions may be-if you ask them to be removed, you are in effect asking to deny yourself the opportunity to learn whatever it is that you are trying to teach yourself. It is precisely because you are so loved and respected by Creation, that It will not deny you the learning that your own soul has ordained.

But all is not lost. You can pray to be shown the meaning of your challenges, and the floodgates of assistance will open up to you. When you ask to know the meaning of the conditions that plague you, you are not abrogating your role in creating them; you are simply saying that the ways in which you create them are as yet not fully known to you. They are largely buried in your unconscious. You are not begging to be rescued; you are asking for greater understanding and to be shown a way out, so that you can rescue yourself.

To me, this is the most effective form of prayer.

#153 **The Current**

In the past six months my sense of guidance has become very, very strong. I have waited for many years to feel this way. It doesn't mean that I never feel fatigue or fear, or that I have overcome the capacity for self-deception. It means that I can feel the great river of life which flows beneath the webs and delusions of my mind. It means that when these webs ensnare me; there is a knowing, sometimes great or sometimes muffled, which tells me that I have never left the river and that it yearns to embrace me with its deep and abiding flow.

It is from the feeling tone of my thoughts, not their logical content, that I can discern if I am fighting the great river of life, or effortlessly moving with it. And there is nothing "right" or "wrong" about any of this. I have a frame of reference; a palpable, experiential frame of reference, which always guides me back to my own being.

I bow before that which I cannot see nor understand; that vast river of life of which we are all particles. We have never left its embrace because it is what we are.

Whatever we may think or feel, it is what we are.

#154 **The Fountain Of Youth**

Lately I have observed that while my body is getting older my consciousness is getting younger! I'm not talking about the dreaded "second childhood". I am talking about the palpable vitality which comes from liberating myself from the deeply rooted fears and emotional patterns which limit the flow of my Divine Energy.

The real fountain of youth is within! Creative Energy is the most vital force in the universe. As we learn that we are this energy, not the conditioned reactions and beliefs which block it, we naturally feel all the joy, purpose, creativity, hope and excitement that it offers us.

The next step is to fully integrate this conscious vitality into the body. This may take a little time but it is possible. I cringe when I hear friends talk about the inevitability of sickness and old age. Every time you think that thought, you create that condition.

I have been advised to see "old age" as a time of wisdom, not infirmity. Now this is advice I choose to listen to!

#155 **The Glorious Uncertainty of Being**

Your awareness (that part of you which encompasses, but is far greater than the reactions, beliefs, emotions and sensations which make up your ego-based "identity") is inherently "uncertain". It is a vibrating, expanding Energy which cannot be contained by any of the old patterns which you have learned to hold onto to keep you "safe." One of the reasons people have challenges at times like

these is because the energy of pure beingness is accelerating and, in a real sense, it is demanding that it simply be experienced. That sounds easy enough. But the mind rebels at the vastness, the expansive purity of being. None of your conditioned needs or emotional dependencies mean anything within the glory of who you truly are. There is nothing to hold onto and yet, if you can become comfortable with this uncertainty, the beauty of your life unfolds in ways which you have never deemed possible. You don't "lose" your ego. Your ego aligns with Creation and becomes the ever expanding vehicle through which you navigate this earthly dimension.

We do not have to be afraid of our own beingness. When all of the things we cling to to keep us safe are stripped away, we find true safety in the glorious expansiveness of what we truly are.

#156 The Release

Everything hidden is being released now, on the individual and the collective levels. It may not be pleasant and the mind resists, but resistance only makes the experience more painful. The dark, hidden places have got to be revealed, in order for the Light to manifest. The only way to deal with this is to be with these spaces as they emerge. This is the path to freedom. Realize that these spaces are not the essence of what you are, but be with them fully. Simply breathing and allowing the thoughts to be, is a healing balm.

Allow the darkness to be enveloped by your beingness. Soon you realize there was never anything to fear, nothing that ever needed to be protected. Perfect beingness is all there is, all you are or ever were.

#157 Depression

If you are depressed it may be that you are not expressing what your soul chose to express when you agreed to come here, because an aspect of your consciousness is resisting doing so. Your soul expression does not have to be something "grand" in the eyes of the world; but it is indeed "grand" in the eyes of the Universe, even if it is as simple as providing one poor child with a hot meal a day, keeping an elderly person a little further from the edge of despair, or planting the most beautiful flower garden in town!

You ask, "how do I know what my soul wants to do?". I say, "by the joy and the peace it brings you."

It really is that simple, actually. When you are sharing from your gut and from your heart, you start to glow and people start to respond. Your beautiful mind is not abandoned, but it assumes its proper role as intermediary - between you as Creation and the material world - rather than as the starting point.

If I were a doctor this would be my standing prescription for every patient: "Share your heart and soul in the world at least once daily, preferably much, much more."

#158 Ego

We often tend to think of the negative ego as a powerful, bullying force, but nothing could be further from the truth. In reality it is born out of fear and it is fueled by its inability to feel connected to All That Is. The more separate it feels from the Divinity inherent within all life, the louder and more desperate become its cries. It's incessant craving to be noticed is a direct result of its inability to know its own worth.

If an insecure young child came to you for direction, would you put all your efforts into resisting him? Or would you be wise and acknowledge him, maintain good limits, teach by example, and welcome him into a more fulfilling way of life?

So let it be with ego.

#159 Laying Blame

There is nobody to blame for your travails. Every word you have ever spoken, every act, every dream, every song, every prayer, every shout, every angry deed, is a muffled cry to the Energy that gave you life, a longing to return to the Great River which you never really left. And now that this Energy is upon you, a part of you desperately wants to flee, to hesitate at the gate, or to lay blame on somebody else for all your perceived hardships.

Laying blame is the most seductive of human acts. The ghost of self-righteousness wraps itself about you and dances a slow dance, whispering that there are no fears to look at, nothing at all that you must face; all your pain is created by "the other".

In the past perhaps this seemed easier than having to proclaim your own Divinity. But not now. As long as you allow yourself to be seduced, you will never be free. And the day will come when "the other" will be pushed - by the same accelerating Energy that is upon you - to proclaim their freedom, because as Gods we cannot live unfree; it is a violation of what we are...and it will not be sustained.

#160 **The Ride**

Can physical ailments actually be cured by aligning with the current of your own life force? Or is this just woo woo talk; New Age gobbledegook designed to breed false hope and line somebody's pockets?

I can only talk from my own experience; and since my pockets are quite unlined, I don't think anybody has to worry about being taken for a ride.

Correct that. I definitely want to take you for a ride. I want to take you for a ride on the river of your own being; on that wave of energy which is what you are, and which is always accessible in the spaces between your thoughts.

Simply put, I have found that the vibrating, pulsating energy which I experience in the stillness, is incompatible with disease. I don't need to be "cured" and I don't need to be "healed." All my distortions, all the symptoms which have manifested in the physical, are simply swallowed up by the energy of my own being. Given a little time, and allowed to flow freely; this energy is resolving all those areas where it has become congealed, and the physical symptoms that go with them.

I certainly can't claim to speak for anybody else. I can tell you that there is no "right" or "wrong," no "good" nor "bad," and certainly no punishment, involved here. Many incredible people are born with or develop illnesses for reasons that I cannot possibly understand. To imply that they have done or are doing something "wrong" is ridiculous.

For myself, however, the silent space of no-thought came alive one day as a vibrating force. It wishes to move freely. To allow it to do so, I must acknowledge, accept and stop feeding the emotional patterns which block it, and the intellectualizations that embrace these patterns. By necessity, I am learning to do this, and the physical results have been dramatic. The real beauty of it is I don't have to "rid myself" of anything, because the river of life dissolves all limitations in its wake.

#161 Relationships

There is a lot of strain on relationships these days. This is because we are being called to live in full self-responsibility as the light beings which we are. It isn't easy. As with all other aspects of our lives, our relationships reflect our existing consciousness. Most of us have, to some degree at least, learned to rely on our partners to stave off fear. Most of us have traded fear for dependency, more often than is healthy or good for us, or for the people we live with.

Now Creation is demanding that we stand on our own two feet (literally) and no longer rely on our partners to provide us with the deep inner security that only we can provide, as aspects of the Divine. This does not mean the end to companionship or romance, nor does it have to mean physical separation.

But courage is called for, courage and deep self-honesty. Old habits of codependence die hard. But the pressure to break these habits is inexorable and, kick and scream as we may, it is for the highest good of all.

This is not about separation. It is about the Divinity which we are, and which we have summoned unto us. It is about a new way of being in the world.

When in doubt, throw right and wrong in the garbage, and surrender to the heart.

#162 The Most Important Distinction You Will Ever Come Across

Allow me to explain a distinction which may be the most important distinction that you will ever come across in your life. This is the distinction between fully accepting your full range of emotions, and allowing those emotions to define who you are. We all know by now that resisting uncomfortable, disturbing or fearful emotions only makes them stronger. We also hopefully know that it is not in our interest to magnify these emotions, nurture them or act from them.

And so the teachings tell us, from so many Wisdom Traditions, that we must simply observe our emotions and they will pass through us and eventually lose their power.
I would add two points. Firstly, before we can observe we must acknowledge and accept. You cannot observe a bird flying through the sky unless you first accept that it truly exists. Often I find that in our haste to observe our emotions, we do not allow ourselves to truly feel them. This is not healthy because what is not truly felt may come knocking on our door again, in an even more intense form, demanding to be heard.

The second point that I would make is that in addition to accepting the full range of our emotions, we must affirm who we truly are. I like to use the affirmation: "I am a Light Being. As Light I express love. Expressing love, I do no harm." I believe this part of the process takes a little practice and may seem tricky at first. In other words, if you feel like punching someone in the nose, and you say the affirmation I just described, aren't you repressing or denying your emotions? My answer is "No, you don't have to repress anything." The mistake people often make is that they think they have to deny what they are feeling in order to "think positive."

Thinking positive usually comes from the mental level. What I am talking about is more like remembering; really touching deeply into the core of who you are (a spark of Divine love) while at the same time allowing yourself to experience the broad range of your human emotions. With practice you begin to experience your consciousness from what is often called your "awareness." You fully accept and observe your emotions (even the ones that terrify you), but more and more you do that from a space of peace, of memory, of knowing; as if you were watching a play in which you had the starring role. It may start with a simple affirmation, but it grows into a palpable memory of your Divine nature.

I think it is so important to "get" this because so many of our physical and emotional problems come from the fact that we are either repressing our emotions, or we are magnifying them and allowing them to terrorize us. The alternative is to fully accept them and at the same time, remember the fullness of our being. If you say, "That sounds nice, but I have no clue what I am in the fullness of my being, no frame of reference," then simply start with the closest statement you can make to describe your essence. Your soul already knows the words. :) Then as you practice this, you may find that in time you no longer even need the words. You just remember. You move through the world from this space of remembering. And everything else becomes a play to be observed.

#163 Wahoogazimbo

If you asked me, "do you believe in God," I would have to say that the question has nothing to do with my spiritual path.

I am not interested in beliefs, even those that are fueled with intense emotions. It is not that I believe or disbelieve. I simply find that the question is not relevant to my growth.

I am profoundly interested in what I experience within the spaces between my thoughts. The underlying energy that I experience in these spaces has proven itself to be the foundation for my life and happiness. You may call this Universal Energy, but that too is a concept. I use the term for purposes of communication, but I could just as easily call it Wahoogazimbo and the principles that I am teaching myself would be the same.

I am interested in alignment, in moving life force energy through my physical body, in attuning my thoughts and (often unconscious) emotions to its profound and palpable flow. This energy dissolves all my fears when I open to it. It gifts me with delight, purpose, compassion and inspiration. It is constantly expanding into deeper and deeper levels of awareness.

Yes I admit, I do have a hunch that this is the same force that permeates all of creation, but I spend little time speculating on that.

That belief is not necessary either.

#164 **Stuff**

I don't know about you but I am sick and tired of beating myself up about my "stuff". Everybody's got "stuff". I'm sure Jesus and Buddha had "stuff". Your guru (if you have one) has "stuff". "Stuff" is a part of being human. It is what we created this place and these bodies to shine through. A lot of our worldly leaders who pretend not to have "stuff" are getting badly burned when their "stuff" shows up and is plastered all over the evening news.

I am a petty, angry, self-pitying, arrogant, insensitive, obsessive, crazy person who wants to be loved. I am also a magnificent, creative, compassionate, self-sufficient, loving, kind and decent man who stays true to his calling regardless of what anybody thinks of him. Both of these guys are hanging out in the same body. I happen to believe (but can't prove) that the last guy is a more accurate representation of my energetic essence (the vibration of Light), and this thought keeps me sane. This doesn't mean that the first guy is "bad" or "evil"; he just came into being as a result of a bunch of conditioned responses to many wounds, both "real" and imagined. In the deepest sense, I understand that neither of these guys actually exists. They are both constructs, part of how we navigate this dimension. Even if you don't believe that one guy is a better approximation of my deeper essence; I think you have to admit that the second guy is a whole lot happier (and definitely much more fun to be around).

We all know about meditation and allowing the thoughts and emotions of guy #1 to pass through us. It seems to me that another way of consciously aligning with our energetic essence doesn't get as much attention. I am referring to taking action which expresses that essence, that vibration of Light. Instead of fretting about all your stuff - write a poem, sing a song, kiss your cat, hug your friend, go for a walk, relish a nice meal - express that essence into the world in the best way you can. Suddenly you may discover that your "stuff" was just that: a bunch of stuff…that has nothing to do with who you really are.

#165 **Your Uncomfortable Thoughts**

You do not have to go to war with the thoughts that make you uncomfortable. Denying them or judging them as "bad" only causes you to resist them more which in turn just makes their hold on you even greater. If you fully acknowledge them, then you can ask them what message they are trying to bring you and learn to apply that message in your daily life.

For example, let's say you find yourself getting very resentful of your spouse. Now you can deny the fact that you are feeling resentful, insist that you are unconditional love (which is true btw), bemoan your thoughts as being "unspiritual," deny that they exist, ward them off, act them out, or try to escape through some physical pleasure; but at the end of the day the thoughts - and the emotional "juice" which fuels them - remain as strong or stronger than ever. But what if you ask, not in an obsessive or intellectual way, but in an honest open hearted way, "What is really going on here?" Then you feel the answer with your heart and your awareness as opposed to your mind. You might be surprised at what answers you will get fromt the deepest parts of your being. For example, you might find out that you feel your spouse is not giving you much attention lately and you are feeling very alone in the Universe. This might really terrify you. The fear of being all alone, of being abandoned, of being unsafe, could be the primary factor in your resentment. You are angry at the person who you feel you have always relied on to feel safe, and who seems to you to now have other priorities.

Or you might sense that there is some kind of a deep shift going on, that you and your spouse are reaching the end of your "agreement" this life and this is both liberating and terrifying. Your ego cannot bear to admit this so the fear gets magnified into anger or resentment and you don't even know where these feelings are coming from.
The conditioned human reaction is to label our feelings as "good" or "bad" and then go to battle against the "bad" ones (or get depressed and feel guilty about feeling them). But that whole paradigm misses the essential question: What is really going on here, and what do I truly desire, at the deepest levels of my being?

Once you get the message, you now have an extremely liberating and empowering tool that you can use in your daily life. The real key is your intention; everything else is just technique. So when your anger comes up, instead of immediately labelling it as something "bad" that has to be fought against - you can look at it, and just observe it from a deeper perspective. You can even say to yourself, whenever it rears its head, "Ah yes, I am afraid. I am afraid that I am being abandoned and I will be all alone in the Universe. I see now - without any self-judgment - that I am resentful of the person who I feel is abandoning me; resentful because I am so scared."

Then you take it a step further. You say, "Thank you for giving me this message, and now I am going to resolve this issue. I am not going to resolve it by lashing out because that is not what I truly desire. I am going to resolve it by facing my fear of being alone and by cultivating the understanding that the Universe is a perfectly safe and loving place. I am going to affirm what the vast majority of the near death experiencers and channelers tell me, which is that I am never alone and I am always safe. Instead of labelling and doing battle with the symptom, I am going to get to the heart of the issue and resolve it. While I am doing so, I am just going to accept the "symptom," observe it, and watch as it loses its power over me. And if you practice this, it will. :)

#166 **A Conversation With My Right Hip**

Today I had a pleasant conversation with my right hip. (The one that allegedly "has" severe arthritis).

"Hey right hip, how ya doin'?"

"Not that great."

"What's the problem, my friend?"

"You know damn well what the problem is, but you don't listen. I have been trying to tell you for years."

"OK, OK," you got my attention. What's wrong?"

"What's wrong is that the energy down here has been stagnant for years! You've got it all congealed, blocked up, frozen. How do you expect me to do my job in this kind of a work environment? I've had it. I'm ready to quit. I'm very close to telling you to take this job and shove it. (And my co-worker on the other side is coming to the same conclusion)."

"Oh no, I'm sorry, I really had no idea. What caused this ?"

"You went to Yale?? Geez. What do you think caused this? Why don't you ask the brain? Better yet, ask the heart! The heart can tell you better than I can. Your damn fear caused this. All that hesitation, needing everything to be perfect before you dared to express your soul in the world. Always afraid to move forward. Living up in your head and forgetting you even had hips! What the Hell do you expect, man?"

"OK, I get the message. What do I do now?"

"Well you can start by thanking me for giving it to you. Then you can forget all that idiocy that the doctors are laying on you about how this "condition" somehow emerged independently of your consciousness. And for God's sake, do you realize what the word "incurable" does to my cells whenever I hear it?"

"Then you can begin to visualize what you really desire. See us running along the beach together, walking the dog in the woods, twerking your brains out in the living room. This is going to take a little while, because I know how you humans are with your illusion of time. So whenever I complain, instead of thinking you have a "chronic" condition and whining about it, just thank me again for giving you the message, and affirm that you hear me and that we are now getting the energy flowing. Take some risks too, for Christ's sake. Stop waiting for everything to be perfect before you get off your butt. Get out of your damn comfort zone once in a while. And every spare moment, imagine that energy flowing down through me into the earth. If you still feel you need to see the auto mechanic (I'm sorry, the surgeon) after we have done this for a while; at least you will know that you are in charge and that you are getting to the root of the problem."

"I feel a whole lot better already. Seriously, I really do. Thank you, hip. I love you."

#167 Experiencing Your Thoughts From The Expansiveness of Your Being

At times I can spend a long period just observing my anxious thoughts from the perspective of the expansiveness of my own being. At such times, I can watch these thoughts as part of a drama that I choose to be an observer to, rather than as who I am. Then I find myself flipping back into getting caught up in the thoughts again.

I am beginning to see how the dynamics work: the key is that I get seduced by the emotions associated with the thoughts. In other words, if you have a thought which says, "you're a hypocrite and nobody cares what you think," or "I am fat and ugly," - if all you had was the thought itself without the emotional juice behind it-it would have no impact on you. It's the emotional charge that sucks you in and makes you believe that it is real. So the key is to look at that emotional component square in the face, and without repressing, denying, warding off, or magnifying; just say, "Yes, yes, yes I understand this is how my ego works, this is the kind of stuff my psyche throws up at me. There are probably all kinds of underlying things going on; but I still choose to experience all this from the full expansiveness of my being. It is something I am observing, but it is not who I am.

#168 **Resistance**

There is a part of you that resists, that lurks in the shadows, terrified of your greatness. Do not expect it to announce itself, for that is not its way. It prefers to be cloaked in mystery, revealing itself in seemingly unrelated symptoms or moods. It is as much a part of your human life as your yearning. Indeed, without it, there would be no yearning.

It is only through understanding that this beast is tamed. You know you cannot drive it from the fields of your consciousness. You have exhausted yourself trying.

One day you come to the realization that the beast is not a thing apart, that the body has not gone rogue, that you did not just "catch" something. This is not how the universe works, no matter what your mind might tell you. What you have "caught" are your own deepest, darkest fears, returning to you in physical form, begging to be acknowledged and released.

Let us shift our perspective here and now. Let us see pain as a messenger, and let us walk together on the path to freedom.

#169 **Being In The Body**

When I was young I used to spend many hours trying to get out of my body.

Now I spend most of my time trying to get back in.

#170 **Inconsistency**

Many of us feel plagued with inconsistency in our spiritual growth. We may feel wonderful, in tune with our own being and full of love one day, but mired in frustration, anger and doubt the next.

What causes this shift in our emotional state? I find that most often, to use a common phrase, it is something that "triggers" us. Of course in reality nothing outside of us has that power, so the more accurate way to describe what is going on is to say we react and trigger ourselves. This doesn't mean that we are doing anything "wrong." It means that we are in the process of teaching ourselves that we can still be who we know we are, in any situation we come up against. In actuality, we often learn we have this power by reacting, and then discovering that the effects of our reactions are not what we truly desire, or who we truly are.

We learn that, no matter how seductive the reactions can seem (and how "justified" our minds may say they are), if they do not express our soul's deepest desire, we can let go of them and replace them. By making this choice over and over, we stop being buffeted about by forces that we perceive as outside of our control, and we become the Masters of our own consciousness.

#171 **Creative Energy**

There is an energy which exists beyond emotion, beyond physicality, beyond intellectual thought, which realizes all of our individual and collective dreams. It is far more profound than what we refer to as intuition. It is not some abstract concept or fringe belief, but the deepest and most practical power one can ever know.

When, through deep acceptance, the emotional and mental debris are allowed to transform; all that needs to be done to experience this power is to fully engage in the moment. The energy will attract everything you ever desired or needed to fulfill your soul's design in this world. You control the pace of your conscious experience of this force by the degree to which you are able to live fearlessly.

Just because this energy is not yet fully acknowledged does not mean it isn't real. It is inexorably making itself known to every living thing. You can cling to worn out ego structures and beliefs, but you will not escape its impact, as you see the things you cling to unraveling before your eyes. Or you can ride this wave and find that there is no end to the purpose and excitement its expansion offers you.

You already have everything you need. It is all contained within the great river of life, waiting to be released into form.

This is not fantasy.

This is evolution.

It is real and it is now.

#172 **Your Fears**

Don't just acknowledge your fears, **experience them;** breathe deeply into them, even if they make your teeth chatter and your legs grow wobbly. This is **not** the same as magnifying, nurturing or acting on them. And it certainly is not the same as denying them, running from them, or trying to "cure" them. This, I believe, is where most people get tripped up. We become so intent on making our fears go away, that we never allow ourselves to experience them and receive the message that they are trying to give us.

But there is more to this process of transformation. As you breathe deeply into your fear and feel it fully in your mind and in your body; choose to experience it from the fullness of your consciousness. You don't try to change the fear; you just begin to remember the rest of what you are.

The fear is a tiny sliver of your consciousness, masquerading as the whole. You remember the fullness of what you are by relaxing, breathing deeply, allowing a good friend to remind you, letting music touch your heart and soul, standing on the earth, petting the dog, or just affirming it with a silent statement. The fear may tell you that it is the true reality, and none of these activities will help you. Just accept that this is how fear behaves and do whatever you have to do to bring your full consciousness to bear.

You are, dare I say, changing the paradigm. It's like you have a jar of dirty water. Instead of becoming obsessed with how dirty it looks and focusing on this day and night; you bring it to the ocean. The ocean can handle it. From the perspective of the ocean the dirty water in the jar is minuscule. And believe it or not, the dirty water is thrilled when it is finally allowed to escape from the prison you have kept it in and is allowed to be transformed by the ocean.

There is some very, very good news here friends. The good news is that, as you practice actually allowing yourself to experience your fear (or your anger, or you depression, or your guilt) and -instead of fighting it or trying to make it go away- you just just bring the fullness of your consciousness to bear on it, the negative emotion loses its power. The emotional "juice" dissolves on its own over time (and it does not have to take a long time either)!   Just remember that every time the fear comes up, if you let yourself feel it and just ask to experience it from the fullness of your being, the fear is dissolving a little more.

One more thing. This may go against a lot of New Age thinking, but I say, "respect your fear." I say this because your fear did not arise out of thin air to torment you. Your fear is an attempt by your human consciousness to get your attention. It is a messenger. There is something that you may not have wanted to look at, some conflict that is only partially conscious, some war going on within yourself; and your fear is pointing back to that. You don't have to analyze this in great detail or get obsessed with it. But it might be something to feel out in your meditation, when you thank your fear for giving you its message.

#173 **Illness And Health**

I am deeply saddened by the fact that the vast majority of people are convinced that illness is the "luck of the draw"; that it arrives out of nowhere to attack the human body. Even those who understand the material connection between lifestyle, nutrition and health, often believe that certain diseases or conditions are "caught" for no valid reason. I believe, based on my deepest sense, that whatever diseases or "conditions" I experience, are physical manifestations of patterns of energy which are, to put it simply, not flowing freely.

I do not claim to speak for anybody else. We are holistic beings, and by that I mean that the mental, physical, emotional, and energy levels are interwoven. So when energy congeals, there are "negative" emotions (often barely conscious), beliefs, and physical symptoms all occurring at the same moment. This, it seems to me, is one of the reasons it is often such a challenge to heal. We can say affirmations all day (and I firmly acknowledge the power of affirmations) but if that is all we do, we may be working primarily on the mental level only. We can dig deeper and stop nurturing those emotions that do not serve us by relaxing, letting go, and refocusing (all of which I highly recommend). But if we still believe that life is an endless struggle, and the best we can hope for is to manage our suffering, than this belief will work against all our best efforts to balance ourselves emotionally. If we dedicate ourselves to the mental and emotional levels but decide that the physical can be neglected because "we are not our bodies", then the demands our bodies place on us may make it very difficult to deal with life. And if we ignore the most important level of all, the Divine Energy which is what we are, by not grounding it or helping it to flow; we undermine everything else.

Stand on the earth, consciously move your energy through your body, lovingly observe and let go of the stories that do not serve, cultivate optimistic and positive beliefs, honor your body with the foods that sustain it, dare to create what your soul cries out to create, surround yourself with people who are able to honor you, and fill your mind with the works of those who truly inspire you. I have found that our prayers are answered when we dare to break through the illusions of our alleged limitations. Just the tiniest crack is all the unseen helpers need, but first we have to give them the opening.

#174 God And The Devil

I don't need a concept of God to describe what it feels like to be aligned with my own being, and I don't need a concept of the Devil to describe what it feels like not to be.

#175 Manifesting

Sometimes the ego's desire to impose its agenda on a situation can be quite subtle. It knows full well what you long for since it has been accompanying you on this journey for a very long time.

The surest way to know when the ego is raising its head, is to honestly be with the feeling tone of your thoughts. The feeling tone of your thoughts will let you know if you are really being honest with yourself. While the mind is easily enlisted in the service of the ego, your feelings will tell you, "wait a second, something is a little off here. This just doesn't feel right".

The ego whispers, "you need this and I will show you how to get it". It is quite easy to be seduced by these whispers because the ego understands your deepest longings – for creative expression, for community, for relationships, for resources - but it doesn't have a clue as to the most effective way to manifest them. Manifesting what you truly desire does not come from a sense of lack or need.

It does not require you to impose your will on anyone or anything. It comes from being aligned; aligned with the space of harmlessness, joy and compassion which is your deepest essence. The ego is not a bad fellow really. He is just stuck in permanent survival mode. When he raises his lovely head there is no need to whack him; just give him a little pat and let him know that he has been heard.

When you access the space of your deepest being, things start to happen magically. You aren't making them happen, they just happen.

Everything you have ever wanted is within you, waiting to be born.

#176 **Beingness**

In our incompleteness, we seek the perfect man or woman to bring us happiness. The great irony is that when we surrender to the current of our own being and quit seeking, he or she may actually show up. We seek the resources we think we need to survive because we feel unsafe and alone. When we learn to flow within the river of life we realize that we have always been safe and never alone. As we rest in the abundance of All That Is, resources start to flow to us from the most unexpected quarters. We seek fame or material success because we feel a deep sense of unworthiness. When we touch the hem of our Divinity, nothing can ever make us feel unworthy, and the world responds as it would to an honored guest.

The mind holds us tightly in its grip and uses all the logical tools at its disposal to convince us that our beliefs are real. We were never taught the profound importance of aligning with our own Divine nature. From the moment we took our first steps we were told we had to struggle. In our struggling, we lost touch with the beingness that is what we are; the space from which all abundance flows and all dreams are realized.

#177   **Evil**

Whenever anybody talks about destroying evil, this usually means great "evil" is about to be unleashed.

#178   **The Power Of Thought**

The power which a thought has over you is in direct proportion to your refusal to truly feel it.

#179   **The Symptom Is The Message**

As hard as it may be to accept at times, the fact is that the symptom is the message. We are taught to view the symptom (emotional or physical) as the enemy, and most of modern medicine is designed to blot it out, one way or the other.

Now I will be the first to admit that there are times when it is just too challenging to get the message and allow the symptom to transform. This is when direct manipulation of the physical may be necessary. But at these times it is more important than ever not to lose perspective. Your sleeping pills will not reveal to you why you can't let go into the nurturing beauty of sleep; your antidepressants will not tell you why you are blocking your inherent joy, your heart meds will not explain what is wounding your heart in the first place. The list goes on and on. Of course there may be reasons that only a soul knows for why various symptoms develop, and you are never doing anything "wrong." But in most cases the message is pretty clear, if we are really honest about our feelings, our desires, our beliefs and, of course, our fears.

The problem with bludgeoning the symptom is that you usually have to pay the piper, sooner or later. Using the drug long term may end up worse than the symptom it is trying to obscure. Covering up one problem may result in a totally new problem coming out in a different area of the body. A true healer will help you to understand the deeper issue that you may not always want to look at. And I am not talking about extensive psychotherapy; I am talking about simple tools to help you find out what your body and your emotions are really trying to tell you.

Modern medicine certainly has its place but I suggest you use it wisely. Do you really think it is wise to surrender yourself to people who may barely know who you are? How can they truly decide what is best for you if they do not know your deepest yearnings, your profoundest dreams, your sacred loves and your darkest fears? Don't all these things play a central role in your healing?

Today if a doctor tells me he or she has been practicing medicine for forty years, I tell him that I have been residing in this body for 66.

If he doesn't understand the importance of that little fact, I give him my blessings and walk out the door.

#180 Heaven On Earth

When we stop trying to make things happen because we don't love ourselves enough, and we release our obsession with survival; we access that mighty river of life where all of our dreams flow endlessly. When we can no longer resist the sweet calling of these dreams, Heaven appears on earth; first in our own lives, and then in the whole world.

#181 **The Trick**

The trick, it seems to me, is to fully accept and feel all of your reactive emotions (fear, guilt, shame, rage, anxiety, etc.) without being seduced into experiencing these as the core of who you are. Denial doesn't work, resistance doesn't work, self-judgment doesn't work, pretending doesn't work, magnifying doesn't work, acting out doesn't work; but remembering that at your core you are compassion, joy, creativity, etc. does work. But it only works if you truly believe it and if you fully accept the full range of your emotions, and simply observe these without allowing them to overtake your experience of Self. All the great teachers that I know of tell us the same thing about who we are at our core, and that is Divine Energy (or unconditional love).

It's a neat trick, this shift in perspective. It allows you to view your reactive self as if you were watching a play with that part of you in the starring role. (You can even describe the scene if you like: "There goes Ted again. He feels like his support system is eroding. His obsessive mind is really going off because he is scared and his body is feeling under pressure. Poor lad. Pass the popcorn, please)". :)

There will be big challenges, but the reward is freedom; freedom from confusion, freedom from anxiety, freedom from guilt, freedom from isolation, freedom from despair; as the reactive emotions loose their grip over you. This, to me, is the detachment of which the Masters speak. It is not about detaching yourself from your desire for a new car (which can be a balanced expression of your core). It is about learning to detach yourself from the deep emotional pull which your shame, guilt, rage, fear and obsession have on you; not by denying or judging these emotions as good or bad, but by calling forth the deeper part of your being and observing them from this space.

For most people, being "true to themselves" means experiencing whatever emotions and reactions they happen to be having at the time, as constituting the center of their being. I suggest that being "true to yourself" really means fully acknowledging and accepting all these emotions without judgment; but still experiencing (or at least remembering) the core of your being for what it is; a spark of Divine Energy.

And I promise you it gets easier to do this as you practice it. :)

#182 Ode To Fear

My dear fear. How you love to hide in the marshes and reveal just enough of yourself to unsettle me! You infiltrate my knowing with your endless scenarios of self-destruction. Like a prince you conceal your emptiness with the finest garments, but once revealed you dissolve into mist.

I understand you now my friend. You have sought me out one too many times. Eventually even the thick headed become on to your ways. All these eons you have pursued me; and all these eons all I have ever had to do was look at you. Just look at you squarely - not with my head to the ground or my eyes darting side to side - not caught up in the illusion of your mysteriousness. Just stand my ground, breathe deeply, and look at you. Once I mustered the courage to see you, once I stopped running from you and designing plots to destroy you, you graciously dissolved into nothingness. Perhaps, like so many humans, all you ever wanted was to be seen.

I invite you to the feast, my friend, for you have caused me to tremble, and in allowing myself to tremble, I became whole.

#183 Your Sacred Consciousness

I say question the reality of your "illness". Is it solid, is it real? What have you got to lose? It doesn't cost you anything. You don't have to give up your conventional or alternative treatments to do so. The beauty of being out of balance is that you have the potential to get back into balance. It is a process not a "thing". A process can be reversed.

Our deeply rooted emotional patterns can squash our conscious alignment with our true magnificence. This isn't "right" or "wrong". It is a cause for clear thinking; not self judgment. We all do it. It is part of our learning as human beings. Could I really have expected that all of the fear I created, over 65 years, would have no impact on my physical body?

You may say, "Well, this doesn't work; nobody cures themselves". I say, dare to forget everything you think you know about what is possible. This is a new moment in human consciousness. We are reaching the point collectively and individually where "miracles" are becoming commonplace. Perhaps you feel this too, deep down inside. Don't let the chains of perceived possibilities bind you. There are messengers popping up all over the place, reminding us of what we really are, inspiring us to claim our birthright. Yes, they are not in the majority yet, but their numbers are growing.

So again I say, question the assumption that what you call illness is something real and solid, rather than the physical manifestation of a process that you have the power to impact.

Your consciousness is sacred. Please don't give it away.

#184 **Shifting Perspective**

Instead of fighting, denying or magnifying the thoughts and emotions which you don't like, try something different. Step back and say to yourself, "I choose to view these thoughts from the expansiveness of my being." You may use the term "awareness" or "consciousness" instead of being, whatever you feel comfortable with.

What does it mean to make the simple choice to experience your thoughts and emotions from your awareness or being? It means that, to the best of your ability, you get in touch with the joy, safety, purposefulness, beauty, compassion and creativity of the

Universal Energy of which you are a part. Then you simply shift perspective; because the reactive, terrifying, unwanted thoughts are now being observed by you, instead of controlling you or driving you crazy. You have made the decision to watch those terribly anxious thoughts as if you were in a play and you were performing the starring role!

The good news is this really works. And best of all, if you do this for a while (and it doesn't have to be for that long), the destructive or scary thoughts melt away on their own. Remember that ACIM says a miracle is "simply a shift in perception from fear to love." I would say that if you chose to make your stand from the fullness of your being than the love is automatic.

#185 Another Tool For Spiritual Growth

One of the most profound tools that I have to assist me in my spiritual growth is the capacity to understand what my ego is up to.

In the long run, of course, the ego is not "negative," in that it simply brings up those aspects which we are transforming; guilt, self-reproach, obsession, projection, self-pity, hostility, etc.

If we can understand (without analyzing to death) the role that the thoughts or emotions which burden us are playing in our lives; we can go a long way to allowing these thoughts and emotions to lose their charge. I agree of course that "we are not our thoughts." Nevertheless, it has been extremely liberating for me to recognize what certain thoughts and emotions are up to; and to lovingly identify their game as I allow them to pass through me. In so doing I have been able to acquire some precious distance between my experience of self, and those thoughts which come from the "negative" ego.

For example, I will have certain thoughts which can stop me dead in my tracks and make it very hard for me to do the things that bring me joy. With the help of my amorphous friends (The Ones With No Names, channeled by Flo Aeveia Magdalena) I have come to understand that these thoughts are simply my negative ego's way of paralyzing me, of keeping me from moving forward and expressing my soul's deepest desires in the world.

Some of the negative ego's thoughts can be very seductive because they have been such a large part of our consciousness (though often unconscious) for our entire lives. They don't reveal their purpose by saying, "I am giving you this thought to keep you from expanding because I fear expansion." Rather they tell you what a horrible person you are, unable to follow through with anything. It is enormously liberating to understand what these thoughts are up to, and to be able to say to them, when they arise; "ah yes, ego-based thoughts passing through, attempting to keep me from doing what truly brings me joy. I understand you, my friends. I know that the emotions around you are very strong; but I know that you do not represent who I truly am at the deepest levels of my being. I let you go. Thank you for coming to the surface so that you can be released."

This to me, is the true meaning of freedom. It is about being able to tap into the vast reservoir of creative energy at our disposal, without getting caught up in illusions. It is not about right or wrong, how hard we try, or what kind of a person we are. It is about being conscious of what roles the different aspects of our consciousness are playing in our lives. It is about creating distance between how we experience ourselves and the thoughts that come into our heads; so that we assert ourselves as the masters of our own consciousness, instead of being caught in a cycle of reactivity.

This practice is not necessarily something that is accomplished in a day. However, once you begin to apply it, the results can be quite remarkable. It is about getting the message behind the thoughts that make you uncomfortable, acknowledging this message, and watching those thoughts lose their charge.

There is one more ingredient to this process. You need to believe (even if you don't feel it at the moment) that you really are the being you desire to be; that your essence is truly magnificent.

It is you know.

#186 Who Do You Believe You Are?

When a disturbing or negative thought pops up can you just ask yourself a few simple questions? Does this thought express the deepest, truest desire of my being? Does it represent what I truly want, at the deepest level of my soul?" Does it really represent who I truly am? If the answer is no, then just decide to let the thought go. Don't try to fight it. The act of fighting itself is a statement that you believe the thought is true. You only fight things that are real. You don't do battle against ghosts and figments.

So in practice what is the problem? Once we fully decide that a thought does not express what we really want or who we really are, why can't we snap our fingers and immediately let go of it. The answer, in my opinion, is that we are still being seduced by the emotional juices attached to the thought.

Let us say someone puts you down. You start to get very depressed, passive aggressive, or anxious. You start to have thoughts like, "I can never do anything right," "I should just kill myself because I will never amount to anything."

Now if I were to ask you, "Do these thoughts accurately reflect who you truly are at the deepest level of your being?" or "Do these thoughts express the deepest, most authentic desire of your soul?", if you were honest you would have to say, "No, they do not," because you do not feel this way at your core.

The good news is, you can break the hold which these constrictive emotions have on you. You will not do it by denying them, because that will just make them stronger. You will do it by acknowledging them, feeling them, then affirming what you really are. You can affirm it with a statement, or, more effectively, with a statement, a deep breath, and an intention to consciously remember the beautiful, magnificent aspects of your being. That is to say, the truth of who you are.

And the good news is, once you really decide on the truth of who you are, you will simply no longer believe the emotions that are attached to the unwanted thoughts.. It's really that simple. You can spend 20 years in therapy, but you still have to decide the truth of who you are.

IV. SONGS

#187 **The Sapling Tree**

One day while travelling, rambling free
I came upon a sapling tree
Said I, "My friend so small and fair
What thoughts for living can you share?"

"I am a frail and fragile tree
The winds and rains, they buffet me
I yield my body to the gale
Resisting not, I do prevail.

My roots go deeply to the earth
The hallowed mother who gave us birth
My branches are lifted by day and by night
Expressing the Oneness and sweet delight

I have no need for toil you see
Content am I to simply be
Though I wear the costume of a tree
My essence is Divinity."

"Oh Holy, Holy, Holy tree
Your gentle wisdom comforts me
How may I learn to simply be

What is the secret of the tree"?

"Step ye lightly on the land
Give of your grace to every man
Resist not tempest, gale nor storm
Live from substance, honor form

Still your mind to set yourself free
Then let your heart soar heavenly
Feel the earth rise through your feet
That sacred grounding where they meet."

I dropped my body to one knee
And touched the branches of the tree
I felt the force that makes it be
The selfsame force that flows through me

"Oh Holy, Holy, Holy man
I know that now you understand
That I am you and you are me
That was the secret of the tree."

One day while travelling, rambling free
I came upon a sapling tree
Said I, "My friend, so small and fair
What thoughts for living can you share?"

#188 Light And Dark

Light and dark, dark and light
See the world with Heaven's sight
Find the treasure in the night
Light and dark, dark and light

Wheel is spinning, spinning round
Feet can barely touch the ground
Spins the gold that makes the crown
All is lost, all is found

Light and dark, dark and light
See the world with Heaven's sight
Find the treasure in the night
Light and dark, dark and light

In the forest walk alone
Footsteps falling, blood and bone
Feel the heartbeat, hear it moan
Let the terror take you home

Light and dark, dark and light
See the world with Heaven's sight
Find the treasure in the night
Light and dark, dark and light

In the cauldron feel the flames
Let them burn away your name
Sacred ashes all that remains
Nothing ever stays the same

Light and dark, dark and light
See the world with Heaven's sight
Find the treasure in the night
Light and dark, dark and light

#189 I Will Be There For You

When all that you own crumbles and dies
When the truths that you've known turn into lies
When the voice of your lover reveals its disguise
I will be there for you

When the face that you wear cannot conceal
When the pain that you bear is all that you feel
When the world that you touch seems no longer real…

I will be there for you

I will be there in the kiss of the wind
When your heart finds its wings and the music begins
I will be there on the rays of the sun when your chains fall away
And Awakening's begun
When your chains fall away,
Awakening's begun...
I will be there for you

When the walls of your mind wash away like the sand
When the self that you hold to cannot withstand
When emptiness calls but you don't understand...
I will be there for you

When the ones you revere can no longer pretend
That they live without fear, that they're days will not end
When the earth and the waters can no longer bend...
I will be there for you

I will be there in the kiss of the wind
When your heart finds its wings and the music begins
I will be there on the rays of the sun when your chains fall away
And Awakening's begun
When your chains fall away,
Awakening's begun...
I will be there for you

When your name's just a word never uttered with care
When your voice is unheard no one knows you are there
When the world and its treasures yield only despair...
I will be there for you

When you call to your hands but they do not reply
When your body's demands fill the darkening sky
When hope is a shadow and you think you will die...
I will be there for you

I will be there in the kiss of the wind

When your heart finds its wings and the music begins
I will be there on the rays of the sun when your chains fall away
And Awakening's begun
When your chains fall away,
Awakening's begun...
I will be there for you

For yours is the earth the stars and the sun
Hallowed at birth, a gift of the One
Yours is the promise that's never undone...
And I will be there for you

I will be there in the kiss of the wind
When your heart finds its wings and the music begins
I will be there on the rays of the sun when your chains fall away
And Awakening's begun
When your chains fall away,
Awakening's begun...
I will be there for you

#190 The Firefly Song

When I was young, or so I'm told
I gave no thought to growing old
I'd chase the wind to my heart's delight
And dance with the fireflies, through the night

Fireflies, Fireflies
Light up the darkness, thrill my eyes
Sparks of wonder, sparks of love
Scattered by angels from above

Oh come little one and stop your play
Learn to do what others say
Spend your hours on your ABC's
Leave those fireflies to the trees

Fireflies, Fireflies
Light up the darkness, thrill my eyes
Sparks of wonder, sparks of love
Scattered by angels from above

Learn that God is way up there
Learn some words and call it prayer
See the world through grown-up eyes
Forget the dance of the fireflies

Fireflies, Fireflies
Light up the darkness, thrill my eyes
Sparks of wonder, sparks of love
Scattered by angels from above

Now I am old and growing wise
The light flows dimly from my eyes
I see this world was a grand disguise
I'm going home to my fireflies

Fireflies, Fireflies
Light up the darkness, thrill my eyes
Sparks of wonder, sparks of love
Scattered by angels from above

So come my friends, open your eyes
See how reason often lies
We'll form a circle 'neath the skies
And dance the dance of the fireflies

Fireflies, Fireflies
Light up the darkness, thrill my eyes
Sparks of wonder, sparks of love
Scattered by angels from above

#191 **The Lady Of The Light**

The night is still, a birthing moon
Casts its blessings on the earth
I hear her calling in the wind
The angels dancing wild with mirth

In her eyes a million worlds
Are born and slowly die
A silver chalice in her hands
And at her feet the Masters lie

"My son, my son, my precious one
Give me your cup of tears
And drink the nectar of my love
To wash away all ghostly fears."

I stumble to the barren ground
Lost in the cauldron of my will
She bows to touch my trembling heart
A million stars grow brighter still

"Through the ages I have come
To weave my golden thread
And to bind each broken heart
To the dream that we are wed

I have heard each desperate cry
I have caught each falling tear
I have held the promise close
The time of peace that draws so near

And now the veil, it fades and falls
The Quickening has begun
And the eyes of humankind
Look within to greet the One

My son, my son, my precious one
Sweet dreamer of the dawn
Will you hold my lamp aloft
Until all human tears are gone?

Know that I am your very breath
The beating of your heart
And we have danced among the Spheres
In the realms where sorrows part."

The night is still, a birthing moon
Casts its blessings on the earth
I hear her calling in the wind
The angels dancing wild with mirth

#192 **Gossamer And Gold**

If my heart had wings my love
Gossamer and gold
I'd soar across the mountain tops
In search of your abode

I'd light me down so swiftly
By your garden fair
And wrap my wings around you love
And gently hold you there

I know you are an angel
Clothed in flesh and bone
For I can see your wings, my love
Each night when we're alone

They beat upon the pillow
And brush away my tears
They shield me from the night fall
And banish all my fears

How can I be true my love

To one as pure as thee
I am but a mortal man
Struggling to be free

Each day I face the darkness
That tries to hide the land
I weave my way through jagged rocks
And somehow make my stand

She says I am an angel
Gossamer and gold
She feels my wings around her
Each night when we're alone

She says I bring her laughter
And cause her heart to soar
Far across the mountain tops
Where she's never been before

For are we not all angels
Clothed in human form
If we could but believe this
This world we would transform

We'd soar across the mountains
To places far and near
We'd spread our wings upon the earth
And build our garden here

If my heart had wings my love
Gossamer and gold
I'd soar across the mountain tops
In search of your abode

I'd light me down so swiftly
By your garden fair
And wrap my wings around you love

And gently hold you there

#193 Angel's Song

The hills are crowned with glory and grace
The fields are blossoming, heather and lace
What is this touch upon my face?
"Be still, my child, be still"

The trees are robed in garments sublime
They call to me from a place beyond time
Whose wings are these that beat so Divine?
"Be still, my child, be still".

The air is full of wondrous tones
They fill my body and thrill my bones
What is this love I never have known?
"Be still, my child, be still"

Then like a dream or a song that must end
I bid farewell to my dear angel friend
How may I ever find you again?
"Be still, my child, be still."

#194 Sophia's Song

When your days are lost in shadow
All your dreams take flight
I will send my true love to you
Healer of the night

When you human heart is weeping
From you cares untold
She will bathe your broken body
With her chalice gold

"Come to me, Oh come to me"
Sweetly calls you near
To the garden of the lilies
By the waters clear.

When the angry mob condemns you
Like a bitter storm
She will wrap her wings about you
All your fears transform

And when the last wild rose lies deathly
On the barren ground
She will weave her fragrant love song
Through your heart unbound

"Come to me, Oh come to me"
Sweetly calls you near
To the garden of the lilies
By the waters clear.

When the ancient forests tremble
'Neath the blades of man
She will breathe a perfect blessing
On this ravaged land

And when at last the sun bears witness
To her grand rebirth
She will call us to her garden
Mother of the earth

"Come to me, Oh come to me"
Sweetly calls you near
To the garden of the lilies
By the waters clear

#195 **When My Work Is Over**

When my work is over
My earthly days are done
Find me a field of clover
Underneath the sun
Form a circle round me
Softly call my name
Sweetly sing my soul to rise
From this worldly game

I am of the mountains
I am of the sea
I am of the breath of life
That flows eternally

You may lay my body
In sweet Gaia's womb
And say a blessing on my bones
To make the flowers bloom

When my work is over
My earthly days are done
Find me a field of clover
Underneath the sun
Form a circle round me
Softly call my name
Sweetly sing my soul to rise
From this worldly game

How can there be a parting
To friends like you and me?
How can there be an ending
To souls forever free?

Why must there be such weeping
When life flows on you see?
Why must there be such grieving
To greet reality?

When my work is over
My earthly days are done
Find me a field of clover
Underneath the sun
Form a circle round me
Softly call my name
Sweetly sing my soul to rise
From this worldly game

#196 **Daddy's Song**

Close your eyes my darling baby
Let the night surround the day
Daddy's song shall light your dreaming
Chase your worldly cares away

I know the land from which you've travelled
Is far fairer than the earth
But the road is here for learning
With each sacred human birth

As the glory of your spirit
Seems to fade and drift away
Let us take these steps together
To the dawning of the day

May I give you all my loving
May I shield you from my fear
May the blessings of the angels
Comfort you and hold you near

La la la, la la la la la
La la la, la la, la la la

And these gifts that you're bringing

For the healing of the world
In your soul there lies the secret
Let the oyster yield the pearl

May your road be free and happy
May your spirit light the way
As the night becomes the morning
Let the darkness bless the day

V. FINAL THOUGHTS

Much has happened since I first started to compile this book over one year ago. I have been greatly heartened by the individual messages, comments and reviews which I have received from readers. Some say they use the book as a guide, asking a question and then opening it to whatever page they are drawn to. Others leave it by the bed stand and read it before going to sleep; opening to whatever post seems to resonate with them. Still others read it in the more traditional way, from cover to cover.

Recently I had the interesting experience of creating for myself what modern medicine refers to as "atrial fibrillation." At first it through me for a loop, inducing an intense mental fog which left me wondering if I would ever be able to write consistently again, with anything approaching coherency. I am happy to report that at the time of this writing, the symptoms of afib are pretty much non-existent. This has happened without any heart rhythm medications or medical procedures. To me this is my own personal miracle.

I have never abandoned the principles described in this book. (I may forget them from time to time but that just feels like part of the challenge of being human). I have come to the understanding that any pain – emotional or physical – that I have ever encountered has occurred when I have listened to the fearful projections of my mind, and allowed them to take precedence over the inner flow of my being (what I lovingly call the River of Life). Understanding how I created dis-ease or dis-comfort is the first step in allowing those conditions to heal. This happens when I fully accept the uncomfortable thoughts or physical symptoms, understand what they are trying to teach me, and then make some different choices. In time, one begins to experience one's pain from the perspective of awareness; like watching a drama in which you are playing the leading role.

In this edition I have included several more entries that I have found meaningful. I hope that it will provide you with a little comfort and perhaps some useful information as you travel on your human journey.

Blessings,

Ted

ABOUT THE AUTHOR

Ted Slipchinsky has a Masters Degree in Social Work and worked in Community Mental Health for several years. Over twenty years ago he underwent a Kundalini-like experience which continues to this day. His reflections, teachings, stories and songs flow out of this experience.

Ted lives, writes and sings in Chester, VT. For more information about Ted's work, please see www.songsofmysoul.com or join his Facebook Group, "The Other Ted Talks". To listen to samples of his music, or order his CD (Light and Dark), please go to http://www.cdbaby.com/cd/tedslipchinsky.

Made in the USA
Middletown, DE
03 October 2015